MOVING ON FROM MUNRO

First published in Great Britain in 2014 by

Policy Press
University of Bristol
1-9 Old Park Hill
Bristol
BS2 8BB
UK
t: +44 (0)117 954 5940
pp-info@bristol.ac.uk
www.policypress.co.uk

North America office:
Policy Press
c/o The University of Chicago Press
1427 East 60th Street
Chicago, IL 60637, USA
t: +1 773 702 7700
f: +1 773-702-9756
sales@press.uchicago.edu
www.press.uchicago.edu

Reprinted 2015, 2016

British Library Cataloguing in Publication Data
A catalogue record for this book is available from the British Library.

Library of Congress Cataloging-in-Publication Data
A catalog record for this book has been requested.

ISBN 978 1 44731 566 7 paperback

Cover design by Policy Press
Front cover image: istock
Printed and bound in Great Britain by www.4edge.co.uk
Policy Press uses environmentally responsible print partners

Contents

List of abbreviations

APPG	all-party parliamentary group
CAMHS	Child and Adolescent Mental Health Services
CBT	Cognitive Behavioural Therapy
CCG	clinical commissioning group
CEO	chief executive officer
CEOP	Child Exploitation Online Protection Centre
CRCs	community rehabilitation companies
CSE	child sexual exploitation
DCS	director of children's services
DfE	Department for Education
GCSE	General Certificate of Secondary Education
HR	human resources
HWBs	health and well-being boards
ICS	integrated computer services
LAP	learning action partnership
LMCS	lead member for children's services
LSCB	local safeguarding children board
MASH	multi-agency safeguarding hub
MST	Multi-systemic Therapy
NECF	National Evaluation of the Children's Fund
NEET	not in education, employment or training
NESS	National Evaluation of Sure Start
NGOs	non-governmental organisations
NHS	National Health Service
NSPCC	National Society for the Prevention of Cruelty to Children
OCC	Office of the Children's Commissioner
Ofsted	Office for Standards in Education
PSHE	personal, social and health education
RCT	randomised control trial
SCRs	serious case reviews
TCSW	The College of Social Work
UEA	University of East Anglia

UNCRC   United Nations Convention on the Rights of the Child

VCSE   voluntary, community and social enterprise

Notes on contributors

Maggie Blyth is the Independent Chair of Hampshire Safeguarding Children Board and the Isle of Wight Safeguarding Children Board. She has held public office as a member of the Parole Board for England and Wales since 2005 and the UK Health Professions Council since 2010. Maggie was a senior civil servant at the Youth Justice Board until 2005, with oversight of policy and practice across all youth justice settings in England and Wales. Her professional background is as a senior manager in social care/probation and previously as a teacher. She has jointly edited five books for Policy Press.

Marian Brandon is Professor of Social Work and Director of the Centre for Research on Children and Families at the University of East Anglia. A qualified social worker, she worked for seven years as a practitioner before taking up an academic post. Her research activity focuses on child protection, children's views of child protection, family support and interagency working. For over a decade, she has directed national analyses of serious case reviews (SCRs) for the English and Welsh governments. She has also worked on studies for the England Office of the Children's Commissioner on children and young people's views of child abuse and child protection and how to improve children's access to early help. She is currently leading a team evaluating family support as part of the Troubled Families initiative for a number of London boroughs.

Eleanor Brazil is currently Director of Children's Services in Doncaster. She is a qualified social worker with extensive experience at director level in both adult and children's services in permanent and interim roles. Her interim work includes the role of Deputy Director in Haringey following the publication of the Peter Connolly SCR, Director of Children's Services in Leeds while in intervention, Director of Children's Services in Birmingham for 17 months until April 2012, and Director of Children's Services in Stoke-on-Trent for a year to assist in its move to a people directorate. She currently chairs the local safeguarding children board in Medway and has been Chair of the Lawn Tennis Association Safeguarding Committee for six years.

Jenny Clifton is Principal Policy Advisor on safeguarding for the Children's Commissioner for England. She is a qualified social worker and has worked in practice, management and lead policy roles in local government and the voluntary sector, with a focus chiefly on children. She has held posts as university lecturer in social work and social policy and has published on children's rights and on domestic violence. Jenny's current work concerns the promotion of children's and young people's rights to protection, their perspectives on the child protection process, and how they might be enabled to access help at an earlier stage.

Brid Featherstone is Professor of Social Work at the Open University. She qualified as a social worker in the early 1980s and has extensive experience of researching service users' perspectives of child protection systems. Her book with Sue White and Kate Morris, *Re-imagining child protection: Towards humane social work with families*, is published by Policy Press in April 2014.

Mark Gurrey is currently working as Director of Improvement for Doncaster Borough Council. He worked as an interim Deputy and Assistant Director in Haringey immediately post-Baby Peter and then in Birmingham and Kent. He is also the Independent Chair of Wiltshire County Council Safeguarding Improvement Board. He is a qualified social worker and started his career as a social worker in Haringey before moving into management in Newham, Hackney, Thurrock and Barnet and then entering the world of interim management.

Charlie Hedges worked for over 30 years as a police officer in the UK. In 1997, his involvement in a difficult missing person investigation where the person was later found deceased made Charlie aware that there was a need to improve police procedures. In 2008, Charlie joined the UK Missing Persons Bureau as Liaison and Support Officer, where he continued his involvement in national policy development and support to police forces at a strategic and tactical level. In 2012, he took up a new post at the Child Exploitation Online Protection Centre (CEOP) as Manager for Missing, Trafficked, Abducted and Kidnapped Children.

Leslie Hicks is Reader in the School of Health and Social Care at the University of Lincoln. She has long-standing research interests in services for children and young people, safeguarding and child protection, and well-being and social inclusion. Much of Leslie's work is underpinned by an interest in organisational dynamics. Her specialist area lies in research related to the experiences of looked-after children and young people.

Ray Jones is a registered social worker with more than 40 years' practice and management experience prior to his current role as Professor of Social Work at Kingston University and St George's, University of London. From 1992 to 2006, he was Director of Social Services for Wiltshire. He was the first Chief Executive of the Social Care Institute for Excellence and has served as Chair of the British Association of Social Workers. He now oversees child protection improvement in four areas across England. He is a frequent media contributor, columnist and commentator, and his most recent book, *The story of Baby P: setting the record straight*, is being published by Policy Press in April 2014.

Kate Morris is Director of the Centre for Social Work at the University of Nottingham. She is a qualified social worker with extensive experience in childcare and protection. Her research interests focus on family-minded policy and practice in care and protection.

Jenny J. Pearce is Professor of Young People and Public Policy at the University of Bedfordshire and the Director of the International Centre: Researching Child Sexual Exploitation, Violence and Trafficking and the Institute of Applied Social Research. She works with Eurochild and the Council of Europe promoting child participation to prevent sexual violence against children. Her research includes studies of gang-affected neighbourhoods, child participation, safe accommodation and child sexual exploitation. She is Associate Editor of the journals *Youth and Policy* and *Child Abuse Review*.

Martin Pratt is Director of Children's Services for the London Borough of Camden. He has over 30 years' experience in the field of children's services and holds a Master's degree in public policy. He is a member of the Council of Reference of the Association of Directors of Children's Services and is Vice Chair of the Board of the Virtual Staff College. He is also a member of the expert reference group for the Child Sexual Exploitation Funders Alliance.

Michael Preston-Shoot is Professor of Social Work and Executive Dean of the Faculty of Health and Social Sciences at the University of Bedfordshire. He is the Independent Chair of Luton Safeguarding Children Board and its Safeguarding Adults Board. His research and writing has concentrated on the interface between law and social work education and practice. His latest book, written with Roger Kline, is *Professional accountability in social care and health: challenging unacceptable practice and its management* (Learning Matters, 2012).

June Thabor worked in local authority social work in England and Canada between 1963 and 1989 before joining the University of East Anglia where she is now an Emeritus Professor of Social Work. Her teaching and research have encompassed family support and child protection services for children and families in the community and services for children in care or placed for adoption. Most recently she has completed a research briefing on children returning home from care for the Social Care Institute for Excellence (SCIE).

Sue White is Professor of Social Work (Children and Families) at the University of Birmingham. She is qualified in social work and was employed as a practitioner and manager in statutory children's services for 13 years. During 2009, Sue served on the Social Work Task Force and subsequently the Social Work Reform Board. From 2007 to 2011, she was Chair of the Association of Professors of

Social Work. She also served on the reference group for the Munro review of child protection in England. She is a currently Editor in Chief of *Child and Family Social Work*. She is a trustee of the Family Rights Group.

Chris Wright is Chief Executive of Catch22. He has over 25 years' experience in the social care and criminal justice environment in a variety of roles, from front-line practitioner to senior manager, and has worked across the sectors and in local and national government. In 2006, he joined Rainer as Operations Director and was influential in the merger with Crime Concern and the establishment of Catch22, serving initially as Chief Operating Officer before taking on the role of Chief Executive in August 2011. He was educated at the universities of East Anglia and Oxford. Chris is an advocate for the social sector playing a key role in the delivery of public services.

Acknowledgements

I would like to thank everyone who contributed to this publication. I am grateful to all the contributors for adding to an important debate concerning children and young people in the child protection system and for expressing their views so candidly and openly about what underpins effective multi-agency child protection arrangements. I would also like to thank Professor Eileen Munro for responding to the views expressed by providing a foreword to the volume.

Foreword

Eileen Munro

When I began to read this book, which reports on progress since my review of child protection, I felt some trepidation. This was not just the understandable anxiety about how good my analysis and recommendations are proving to be in practice, but also because of knowing how the austere economic environment is affecting both families and professionals, creating a harsh reality where children's needs are rising and funding is being cut. The authors here, however, paint a picture that includes reasons for optimism as well as pessimism. Working conditions are indeed hard but people with creativity and determination are making progress in improving the quality of help we provide to children, young people and their families.

The traction that my review has had is because, in the main, it gives public voice to the views held by most about the key ingredients for working well with children, young people and their families or carers. Central to these is the importance of developing respectful relationships with those receiving our services in order to maximise our ability to co-produce improvements in their lives. Previous reforms stifled the creativity and humanity needed by putting too much emphasis on improving practice through standardisation and prescription centrally of what to do. These restrictions have only recently been removed. The amount of central control has been radically reduced and altered in the latest version of *Working together to safeguard children* (HM Government, 2013) and the inspection process has also been revised to focus more on quality and the child's or young person's experience than on compliance with case processing. These changes create more scope for professionals to take charge of their work.

Another basic feature of the work that needs to be sensibly addressed is the unavoidable uncertainty that lies at the centre. As Gurrey and Brazil discuss in Chapter 1, 'confident humility' is the most constructive approach and the public need to learn how difficult it is to do the work well instead of baying for blood when a tragedy occurs.

The changes that can be attributed to my recommendations are, of course, only part of the developing scene in children's services. The authors in this book highlight an emerging policy that may lead to fundamental changes in the way children's services are provided. The current government is keen on reducing the role of local government in providing children's social care, so we may see the increasing involvement of mutuals and not-for-profit and private organisations. Contrasting views on the merits of this are offered in Chapter 2 (critical) and Chapter 3 (approving).

Another area of significant change discussed here is society's growing recognition of the needs of adolescents and the distinctive ways that risk can be evidenced in their lives. Unlike young children, where we are generally concerned with dangerous or inadequate behaviour in the family, adolescents show the impact of maltreatment in their behaviour outside the home, where they may be placed or, to some degree, be perceived to place themselves at risk of harm.

Overall, this book conveys a mixed but realistic picture: a tough environment in which many are managing to keep a focus on driving up the quality of help given to children and young people.

References

HM Government (2013) *Working together to safeguard children: a guide to inter-agency working to safeguard and promote the welfare of children,* London: DfE.

Introduction

Maggie Blyth

About this book

> *It is evident that the harm that children can suffer from living in families with complex problems cannot be prevented by the social care system alone. There must also be a coordinated response from a range of services, including health, police, schools, national policy makers and communities themselves. Together, they must create an environment that supports and nurtures families and challenges and intervenes to prevent unacceptable behaviour.* (Ofsted, 2013a, p 10)

Part 1: Introduction and context

Protecting children from harm is far from straightforward. During 2013/14 we have seen an increased and nationwide focus on the tragic deaths and serious injuries of children across the country and arguably more awareness of the risks facing young people in relation to sexual exploitation and sexual abuse. The public insistence that children should be safe and an understandable shock at the tragic circumstances in which some children die or are seriously harmed has been exacerbated by the number of high-profile serious case reviews (SCRs) published during 2013 (eg Daniel Pelka, Coventry; Keanu Williams, Birmingham; Hamza Khan, Bradford). Of the 133 SCRs under way in November 2013, it is expected that 94% will be published (Association of Independent Chairs of LSCBs, 2013). At best, this has allowed a candid dialogue about the challenges facing front-line professionals and organisations tasked with protecting children from maltreatment and poses fundamental questions for us as a society. At its worst, the requirement to publish SCRs has led to a tide of disquiet from the media and public, suggesting that the focus of these inquiries on 'learning lessons' has become a meaningless mantra. The alarming failures within the system when information is not shared, when teachers, GPs, paediatricians and police officers, as well as social workers, fail to recognise abuse and act swiftly, have become the central story. The fact that in the cases outlined earlier adults deliberately sought to hurt children in their care and ultimately cause their deaths, while successfully deceiving professionals, is a fundamental message lost in most reporting. Instead, criticism has fallen on local authorities, and social care departments in the main, which, as well as dealing with increased workloads, are faced with rapidly diminishing resources. The reality is there is a 26.6% projected reduction in local authority budgets in the five years from 2010 (Institute of Fiscal Studies, 2013). This has been combined with a steady increase in cases referred to the child protection system, with a doubling of core assessments completed between 2008 and 2012 (Department for Education, 2013). In this same period, the numbers of children in local authority care has increased from 59,500 to 67,050 (Ofsted, 2013a). These factors have created a highly charged environment against a backdrop of media statements depicting a failing child protection system that is weak and ineffective. For these reasons, it is difficult to see that the greater transparency sought in publishing SCRs is in any way strengthening the child protection system.

This volume seeks to bring some equilibrium to the limited assessment of the current child protection system post-Munro by exploring some of the reasons behind the challenges facing local authorities and their partners in providing effective child protection arrangements.

At the same time the child protection system is under the spotlight, government ministers have signalled a significant shift in direction in the way that failing child protection services are dealt with. New arrangements are being constructed in Doncaster, where children's services will be delivered by an independent trust, and in December 2013 Birmingham City Council announced a strategy to avoid losing control of its social care department.

In turn, the regulators have raised the bar. In its annual social care report, published in October 2013, the Office for Standards in Education (Ofsted) acknowledges that 'children's social care is characterised by complexity, risk and the responsibility for making decisions that can change the course of a child's life' (Ofsted, 2013a, p 4). At the same time, the regulator is clear that it is unacceptable for authorities to remain 'inadequate' in protecting children and that consistent improvement across the country must be a priority. Ofsted has recognised that many authorities are finding improvement difficult and has responded to this with a new framework for inspection, implemented in November 2013, which includes an offer to support those children's services departments still struggling to succeed (Ofsted, 2013b).

As the contributors here suggest, problems in the child protection system are clear but the solutions can appear convoluted and, most importantly, require strong leadership, including strategic direction locally and nationally. This volume seeks to broaden understanding of the challenges in child protection services and does so in the context of the last major review of the child protection system, the independent inquiry undertaken by Professor Eileen Munro. The final report of her inquiry was published in May 2011 (Munro, 2011) and included a number of recommendations for government and the multi-agency child protection system. She reported on progress against her recommendations in June 2012 (Munro, 2012) and made the point clearly that if her reforms were to have sufficient impact they would need to take account of other extensive public sector reforms under way.

Where some of these changes and indeed the influences underlying work with children and young people are beyond our control, there are important policy implications for children's services and how local authorities, different National Health Service (NHS) bodies, policing and the education sector work together to keep children safe. Those contributing to this volume are consistent in their view that it is vital we critically examine government policy on children's services and that we bring some objectivity to the current 'moral panic' prevalent in the media towards this country's child protection system. This book is about the challenges facing the child protection system nearly three years on from the Munro review. It is also about the obstacles some children face and the extent to which young people are 'protected by those who have ultimate responsibility for shaping the child's world at the level of policy' (Welbourne and Dixon, 2013, p 29).

There are three key themes underpinning this publication. First, different contributors consider the extent to which sector-led system improvements should drive local authority children's services departments, both from a regulatory perspective and in terms of improving outcomes for children and young people. Second, each chapter emphasises the importance of the child's journey through the child protection system – from early contact and referral to children's specialist services to assessment, intervention and receiving help. Attention is given to those groups of vulnerable older adolescents who suffer hidden harm as a result of parental mental health, substance misuse, domestic abuse or sexual exploitation. Ofsted estimates there to be 130,000 children at risk from domestic abuse and 17,000 experiencing harm because of parental mental illness (Ofsted, 2013a).

Third, the volume examines opportunities for reviewing multi-agency working, ensuring closer integration between children's services and other statutory agencies, in particular the NHS, education institutions and policing. As well as asking questions about how services should be delivered on the front line, the volume reflects on whether reduced funding for child protection services will indeed force services to become more integrated and allow more fruitful partnerships between public, private and voluntary sector providers. The book provides an independent analysis of local safeguarding children boards (LSCBs), established in 2006, and questions whether these bodies can provide the level of scrutiny required at local level to critically assess local child protection arrangements.

Part 2: The child protection system

In Chapter 1, Gurrey and Brazil outline the ingredients for improving children's services based on their extensive experience of leading the child protection system out of intervention in different local authorities throughout the country. The chapter argues that sector-led improvement is essential, that effective leadership of the frontline is paramount, and that these should be the key drivers of national policy to improve the child protection system. The authors describe the components of what makes services effective to protect children and attempt to take some of the complexity out of what makes services safe, arguing that this in turn helps front-line staff focus on what is important and will make a difference.

In Chapter 2, Professor Jones sets out some of the factors that have driven change in the child protection systems in England over the past 40 years. His chapter examines policy changes arising from different public inquiries, including the Munro review, and places these in the context of increased activity in the system. He argues that the child protection system in this country is one of the most effective in the world but there are implications arising from the recession and public sector cuts impacting on local authorities, policing and public sector reorganisation, which are manifest in the new NHS architecture and fragmentation of the education system. The chapter considers the unique role of the media in shaping public protection policy across the UK and concludes that child deaths should not be a benchmark of the child protection system. Jones holds the view that there is a demonstrable shift in ethos from the state providing a public service for the most vulnerable to direct contestability from profit-making organisations.

Chapter 3 makes the case for widening the expertise of the voluntary sector into statutory service delivery. Chris Wright calls for a move to open up the market to 'new ways of delivering services and to trust the everyday running and delivery of services to others' (p 69). He shares the view of White, Morris, Featherstone, Brandon and Thoburn (Chapter 4) that services should focus on building relationships with vulnerable families and that other sectors should work alongside social workers in front-line services. It is notable that all four chapters offer clear optimism for improving child protection services and ultimately positive outcomes for vulnerable children and families.

Part 3: The child's journey through the system

Munro coined the term 'early offer' in her review and emphasised the importance of intervening early in children's, young people's and families' lives. She noted that the social work profession had become demoralised, with difficulties in recruiting and retaining staff. She stressed the need to hear and focus on the experiences of children and to refocus work away from bureaucracy and towards strengthening professional judgement. It is notable that it has taken until the latter part of 2013 for the government to appoint a new chief social worker and the establishment of The College of Social Work is a recent development. Whether these reforms will have the anticipated impact Professor Munro expected three years ago is still not clear. Some local authority areas have front-line social work or team manager vacancies of over 40% and the turnover of leadership across directors of children's services is reported to have been running at 32% in the past year (Ofsted, 2013a). Leadership from the centre, as well as stability at local level, is fundamental to any transformation of child protection.

In Chapter 4, Professor White, Kate Morris, Brid Featherstone, Marian Brandon and June Thoburn hold a mirror to the child protection system post-Munro and contend that the unprecedented changes of the past three years are undermined by the failure of organisations to invest in interventions that build on relationships with children, young people and families. They consider some child protection work to have become too divorced from early intervention, with the reality that 'low-level' concerns never meet the threshold for intervention from social care, leading to a lack of services at local level and distrust from service users. They also consider the focus on the child's journey to be at the expense of the wider family. White, Morris, Featherstone, Brandon and Thoburn consider that, despite the questionable impact of early intervention programmes under New Labour, there may be merit in the Troubled Families programme and conclude that 'social work is steeped in managing risk and uncertainty and early help services need this expertise from social work as much as social work needs to connect back with its relationship roots, whether this is within statutory services or in the third sector' (p 86).

Jenny Clifton, in her account of the Recognition, Telling and Help study, commissioned by the Office of the Children's Commissioner during 2013 (Chapter 5) as a direct consequence of the Munro review, reiterates the need for children to form 'enduring and trusting relationships' with adults. She outlines three prerequisites for ensuring that children are seen and heard in the child protection system and places them in a framework of intervention. As with wider children's services, the challenge will be to ensure that those young people most at risk are prioritised in gaining access to universal provision, most notably education and health services.

Dr Hicks, in Chapter 6, reflects that in the post-Munro world, there remains little research evidence on the extent of neglect and queries whether the child protection system is sufficiently tuned to the risks facing adolescents in relation to neglect. Although evidence shows that neglect is the most prevalent type of family maltreatment for children of all ages (Davies and Ward, 2012) and features heavily in SCRs (Brandon et al, 2012), she argues that front-line professionals do not always intervene in the same way they would with younger children. She suggests that 'effective assessment of adolescent neglect needs to build on basic awareness of behaviours and self-care such that differing expectations of appropriateness are made explicit and taken into account when making decisions about providing support' (pp 110–11).

Much of this perspective is echoed in the contribution from Professor Pearce in capturing approaches to tackling risks associated with child sexual exploitation (CSE) and trafficking. In Chapter 7, she argues for a 'conceptual shift' in our knowledge of the child protection system since the Munro review and uses CSE as an example of the 'complexities of extending the child protection framework to embrace the needs of older children, particularly adolescents' (p 125).

In Chapter 8, Hedges claims that while there has been progress in policy on children missing and, more importantly, that policy changes concerning missing children should be inherently linked to those addressing CSE, work remains to be done in understanding the 'continuum of risk' associated with professionals' responses to children missing. Hedges places store on the multi-agency safeguarding hubs (MASHs), or the integrated front-line teams operating a triage system across social care, NHS and policing referred to in Munro's final report (Munro, 2011) and increasingly implemented in different front-line child protection settings. At the time of publication, a Home Office report on the effectiveness of MASHs has been released:

all contributors to this volume are supportive of any reconfiguration of front-line service delivery that enables information sharing and close working relationships between professionals.

Part 4: Strengthening accountability of safeguarding across the partnership

'A major challenge in building a more responsive child protection system is helping a wide range of professions to work together well in order to build an accurate understanding of what is happening in the child or young person's life, so the right help can be provided', writes Munro in her final report (Munro, 2011, p 52).

In light of the difficulties and complexities of multi-agency responses to children, young people and their families who may need support, Munro argued that it is vital that there continue to be clear lines of accountability for child protection. In moving to a system that promotes the exercise of professional judgement, local multiagency systems will need to get better at monitoring, learning and adapting their practice. The government has acknowledged that LSCBs remain uniquely positioned and accountable across local agencies and communities to provide oversight of how the child protection system is working and that they should draw on nationally and locally collected performance information to benchmark performance. From November 2013, LSCBs have become subject to regulation by Ofsted. Michael Preston-Shoot and Martin Pratt (Chapter 9) question whether LSCBs have become a 'symbolic aspiration rather than a systemically informed intention to devise effective systems for addressing the complexities in safeguarding governance' (p 160). The complex accountability arrangements between health and well-being boards, LSCBs and children's trusts can be difficult to understand and, in their view, LSCBs may be found wanting in terms of impact. They provide an interesting challenge as to whether LSCBs can be effective if the child protection system they oversee is subject to a poor Ofsted grading.

This book sets out to understand the challenges that remain for the child protection system in this country by providing different perspectives on policy and practice. It begins with a commentary on wider policy factors, then highlights where practice needs to change to protect the most vulnerable children. It ends with a question about the governance and accountability of the multi-agency child protection system.

References

Association of Independent Chairs of LSCBs (Local Safeguarding Children Boards) (2013) 'Press release: SCRs', 11 November.

Brandon, M., Sidebotham, P., Bailey, S., Belderson, P., Hawley, C., Ellis, C. and Megson, M. (2012) *A biennial analysis of serious case reviews, 2009–2011,* London: DfE.

Davies, C. and Ward, H. (2012) *Safeguarding children across services: messages from research on identifying and responding to child maltreatment,* London: Jessica Kingsley Publishers.

Department for Education (2013) *Characteristics of children in need in England, 2012 to 2013,* London: DfE.

Institute of Fiscal Studies (2013) *2015/16: the squeeze continues,* London: Institute of Fiscal Studies.

Munro, E. (2011) *The Munro review of child protection. Final report: a child-centred system,* London: The Stationery Office.

Munro, E. (2012) *The Munro review of child protection. Progress report: moving towards a child-centred system,* London: The Stationery Office.

Ofsted (Office for Standards in Education) (2013a) *Social care annual report, 2012/13,* Manchester: Ofsted.

Ofsted (2013b) *Framework and evaluation schedule for the inspection of services for children in need of help and protection, children looked after and care leavers (single inspection framework) and reviews of local safeguarding children boards,* Manchester: Ofsted.

Welbourne, P. and Dixon, J. (eds) (2013) *Child protection and child welfare,* London: Jessica Kingsley Publishers.

1

Getting the right things right

Mark Gurrey and Eleanor Brazil

The context

First, a few disclaimers. This chapter does not aim to describe the path to the achievement of excellence or an outstanding service, neither is it a critique of recent or current Ofsted (Office for Standards in Education) regimes and methodologies. It does not offer a road map for those authorities already in intervention – although it is hoped that it may be of assistance to them and indeed to those who feel themselves to be coasting and those waiting for Ofsted and maybe wondering whether they are heading for a fall. Nor is it a blueprint for the design of a social care service for children and their families: we are aware that many authorities are successfully working on this and some are offering very useful models for others to learn from and develop. We make no reference to those developments other than by implication and, as the reader will find, we support models and improvement activities that put good social work centre stage in service development.

Rather, this chapter offers an outline of those areas of any children's system or service that must be addressed if it is to be considered 'safe'. It is based on our combined experience (and that of others working in similar circumstances – the world of turnaround interims in local authority child protection services is small) in several different authorities which have fallen foul of an inspection and been judged inadequate. It sets out a number of organisational characteristics we consider to be key to the provision of at least safe services for children. Weaknesses in these areas were part of our inheritance when we moved to those authorities and needed to be addressed in order to help move those authorities forward.

Necessarily, we set out these areas in a somewhat linear manner. Not only has each area to be attended to and brought in to good order, what is overwhelmingly important is that the interrelationship between each and every one is worked on. If leadership, learning and development, performance management and supervision, and other key areas of service improvement are not all working together and influencing each other, the service response to the complexity of the task will never be what it needs to be or as good as it can be.

Finally, we set out our perspective on the impact of the recent child protection reforms on our view of 'safe' services. In clarifying the different components of what makes effective child protection arrangements, we consider whether the Munro reforms have helped shift practice and the extent to which they have impacted on senior leadership in children's services through the setting of strategic priorities.

Many people will read this chapter and declare its contents to be obvious, self-evident and reflecting what they have been doing anyway. We are sure for most that will be true and we offer our apologies and permission to skip to the next chapter. However, our response might be: how come so many local authorities have been deemed inadequate in recent years, especially those who previously thought of themselves as safe, effective, even good? In our view, this is not simply a consequence of Ofsted setting the bar higher or even too high. It is true that recent changes in the inspection regime have focused more and more on the right things and left authorities with fewer and fewer hiding places. We would agree with the criticism that the Ofsted one-word judgement does scant justice to the complexity of the task but if we are to be inspected at all, clearly it is in our joint interests that the right things are looked at in the right way. We think, in nearly all instances, Ofsted has highlighted weaknesses in some authorities that were both identifiable and solvable.

This chapter is based on what are now considerable joint experiences of working in authorities that were either in intervention, at the beginning of the journey out or had emerged from intervention and moved on. We have discussed this with and learnt from others who have also worked in such circumstances. The content reflects that combined learning and in particular the assessment of what we inherited and the issues needing attention in order to lift all out of intervention. Lest anyone should think otherwise, we are clear that the lifting was not done by us alone; indeed, in at least one instance, all the heavy lifting had been done by the time we arrived. Nevertheless, the learning carries, we believe, both merit and interest.

Speak truth unto power

We take as axiomatic that the safeguarding of children is a difficult and complex business. It is probably one of the hardest jobs in the public sector. Eileen Munro articulated very clearly 'the commonly held belief that the complexity and associated uncertainty of child protection work can be eradicated' (Munro, 2011, p 137). The elements needed to ensure that the job is done successfully must recognise and to some extent replicate the complexity of the task. That is not to say that we need to build a complicated set of institutional arrangements to deliver safe services, but we do need to understand the complexity and in particular to ensure that the elements needed are all in place and working effectively and that the relationships between them are 'right'.

That said, it is our view that the single most important factor is the prevailing organisational culture and, by extension, the nature and quality of leadership in the service.

Safe and effective children's services can only flourish in an atmosphere characterised by openness and transparency, by a willingness to have those 'courageous conversations', to challenge new clothes on the emperor and to raise the difficult and sticky questions that leaders often hope will be left unsaid. If it is true – and we firmly believe it is – that aspirations for the quality of external service delivery are reflected in the internal values and culture of the organisation, then, by definition, organisational culture is key to delivering effective safeguarding for children.

One of the core expectations of social workers is that they will ask those really difficult, challenging, embarrassing and intimate questions that are essential to knowing how safe it is for children in the family. Social workers have to find ways of talking about things that are ordinarily kept private and hidden from public scrutiny, that explore the very heart of family life and lie at the centre of people's views about themselves. It is probably one of the most difficult conversations any public sector employee is asked to have with service users of any description. It is, however, these conversations, held empathetically and sensitively, that form the basis of assessments, care plans and ultimately judgements about the single biggest intervention the state can have in family life: the decision to remove children or not. The consequences of getting these conversations wrong are well known. Many of the recent too-well-known serious case reviews (SCRs), including those covering the circumstances leading to the tragic deaths of Peter Connelly and Keanu Williams, comment on missed opportunities to have and act on such conversations.

Good managers will always be alert and attuned to whether these conversations have been had or avoided, whether the 'quiet knock on the door, no one in' syndrome extends to interaction with the family. This is especially true in families who are resistant or aggressive in their responses. These are sometimes genuinely frightening conversations, particularly where a parent is constantly and stridently verbally (and sometimes physically) abusive, and difficult where parents provide potentially plausible alternative explanations, such as those provided by the mother of Daniel Pelka. But it is the role of the manager to find ways to enable them to happen.

The implications for organisational culture become, we hope, obvious. How much harder is it to have those conversations with families if the day-to-day experience of staff in their organisation is characterised by fear, denial or lack of interest, by a wish to bury bad news? They simply will not happen – and as a consequence the impact on child safety becomes manifest. We have worked in authorities where senior managers were barely visible, even where they occupied the same building as their front-line staff. Equally, we've known places where a request to the resource panel felt worse than going to the dentist, and managers knew that and relished it because ... well, who knows?

Do what you say on the tin, show evidence of congruence between word and deed, work internally as you wish services to be delivered externally, walk the talk. Describe it as you will. But, however described, the culture and leadership of the organisation remains the key single most important factor in building effective safeguarding services. Social workers are very astute in identifying the gaps between the walk and the talk and as soon as they feel they are in an organisation lacking that congruence, the culture is lost. Good directors and assistant directors know and understand their staff, and they also know and understand the difficult judgements that complex cases require. In his report on Doncaster children's services following the publication of the full SCR of the Edlington boys, Lord Carlisle commented positively on the knowledge that the then assistant director had of individual cases. However, what he did not reflect on was the need to balance that with the equally difficult task of implementing good systems and support (covered later in this chapter).

At the heart of the culture must be an agreed and constantly stated and restated sense of what good social work looks like. From our perspective, the fact that government accepted all the recommendations in Munro's final report in 2012 and that her reforms have become a central plank of local authority arrangements and Ofsted regulation is indicative of the fact that she recognised most of what lay behind effective child protection arrangements. What has been most effective about the reforms in influencing improvements in children's services has been the renewed focus on the impact on children in her description of a child-centred system and how to deliver improved outcomes through delivering better early help, improved assessment and analysis, and timely decision-making.

Leadership, organisational culture and all the other factors we touch on later are not ends in themselves, of course. They are means to an end and that end must be the delivery of good-quality social work, which entails setting out what that means and what it looks like. We have worked in authorities where the definition of 'good' has been based on form-filling or timeliness or more generally on the 'mechanics' of social work. Our view, and that of many others, is that definitions of 'good' are rooted in the quality of relationships built with people, direct work skills and creativity shown in driving change in families (most of which is not evident in the completion of forms). It has become something of a cliché to talk about what 'good' looks like – even Ofsted wants to know how it is defined and delivered in local authorities (as set out in the recent Ofsted [2013] framework). Again, this is not simply a question of writing it down and certainly not a question of simply telling people, although both might be necessary. Parenting classes often talk about the benefits of 'descriptive praise'. Simply saying 'well done' is not always enough; it is necessary to say why something was good – how the behaviour sought by the parent was achieved by the child – and the same is necessary here. So, examples of 'good' need to be highlighted, to be shared and accompanied by clarity about why 'it' is as required. The analogy is not perfect, of course, because the basis for this chapter is the adherence to adult–adult relationships not parent–child ones, but it does serve a purpose. It is important in setting out what is good and what is not and reinforcing the former while specifically criticising or discouraging the latter. Definitions of 'good' do not solely reside with managers and leaders: good organisations will be characterised by the ability, indeed expectation, that front-line staff will contribute to, if not lead on, those definitions. If you are still wondering what 'good' looks like, consider this recent message from a head teacher in Doncaster about one of our social workers:

> Yesterday, we phoned for advice regarding a family with suspected physical abuse. The social worker, K, dealt with the situation brilliantly. She was caring and supportive to the children, whilst being informative and empathetic to myself and my staff. K even phoned me at 10:10 pm to inform me where the children were for the night, and again this morning (on her day off) to see how the children were in school.

> K worked a very long day yesterday and didn't even stop for something to eat. She really did show dedication beyond the call of duty.

Having set out how 'it's going to be round here', that must be evident in all you do – whether work on budgets and savings, human resources (HR) decisions, placement and case-based decisions. Everything needs to reflect those stated values. A periodic workshop and the issuing of a mission/value statement will not do it. These have their place but will count for nothing if social workers experience their managers as absent or invisible, if communication up the organisation is hard and anxiety-provoking, and if decisions are simply not made or are made in ways that leave practitioners with the problems unsolved.

Our view is that the Munro review has helped set the scene for this approach. She has, of course, shifted the focus back to the child and to the importance of building relationships, helping people change and simply helping people. However, we think that not enough attention is given explicitly to leadership and culture, which we believe to be central – hence our leading on it here.

Confident humility

All of the foregoing requires a certain approach, a certain style from leaders that describes what they do and how they expect others to behave. Googling 'confident humility' shows its roots in both religious and management teachings. For us, it captures the very heart of what makes for a good leader – and what makes for a good social worker. The mixture of confidence born of experience, professional knowledge and expertise, of academic learning and research combined with the humility to recognise there is always more to learn, that we can all get things wrong, that other people (wherever they are in the organisation or the family) may know something we do not, and the willingness and ability to step back from and review a position – all describe a good leader and a good social worker. Any organisation that is at least in part characterised by senior officers who believe or give the impression that they know everything and are always right simply by dint of their position will not encourage social workers to adopt the necessary position of confident humility with families.

Aggregation of marginal gains

So, leadership and culture rooted in the definition of good social work standards are, in our view, the single most important factors in a children's social care organisation. They are not, however, the only ones; there are a range of other matters that need to be addressed and attended to in order to deliver good services. When we were in Haringey post-Baby Peter, our mantra was that there was 'no one thing that would fix it' (this was covered by a *Guardian* interview with Eleanor Brazil in February 2010). Progress was required simultaneously on a whole raft of interconnected but separate fronts, which moved them forward both individually and collectively. Sir Dave Brailsford coined the more elegant term, 'aggregation of marginal gains', to capture the same sense of needing to attend to every aspect of service development (or, in his case, every aspect that gives a competitive advantage), to ensure that each is as good as it can be in and of itself and that it makes sense of and contributes to the whole.

What we now would argue is that there are a number of relatively limited areas that are absolutely key to maintaining a safe service, or rebuilding a broken one. They might find their manifestation differently in different organisations but, at heart, they are constant and essential.

(a) Quality assurance and performance management

It remains remarkable that some services have poorly developed or even non-existent quality assurance systems in place. What is perhaps even more astonishing is that some services appear actively to avoid looking into the darkest corners of their organisation for fear of what they might find there. Those are the places where the light needs to be brightest and any service that stops shining the light will quickly slip into difficulties. Not turning over stones for fear of what is underneath is a policy doomed to failure: you turn over stones because you do not know what is underneath them. The failure to shine the light and turn over the stone will rarely, if ever, be a stated policy, of course. However, senior managers and members who only want to hear good news and performance successes are doing exactly that and they are more common than they should be. It is the duty of others, especially those at assistant director level, to ensure that bad news, the data showing poor performance, is exposed

—

and shared; doing so makes that person more not less secure in his or her position.

This is not the same, or at least should not be the same, as an obsession with numbers and data at the expense of all else. Much of the data we collect are not genuine outcome data and tell us little about what impact we are having on individual children. What they do tell us is something about how well our systems are working and whether the processes necessary to improve outcomes are in place and being delivered. An intelligent look at data should lead to a constant questioning of how children are progressing through the service and with what kind of outcomes. These hypotheses then need to be tested by case-auditing systems. We have been in places where there have been no audits undertaken. We have been in others where anything that moves, and some things that do not, has been audited. Neither, of course, is very helpful or informative. Audits should fulfil one of three purposes. First, they offer some internal independent view about the progress of a particular case and give managers and practitioners the chance to learn on that case and the opportunity to take any necessary remedial action. They give managers much-needed insight into how individual practitioners are practising, who is struggling and who is achieving well. Second, when aggregated together, audit findings give some overview about how a service is performing and how certain aspects of that service are doing. Audits might reveal a common and repeating weakness around supervision or direct work with children, or quality of assessments. The important thing, of course, is to feed that learning into the next phase of service development to ensure that the improvement cycle keeps turning. Finally, audits should help answer specific hypotheses generated from an intelligent look at data. Oddities in conversion rates or data out of step with their statistical neighbours may or may not be something to worry about – one only knows by looking at a sample of cases where one's hypothesis falls.

Audits should also tell us something about the quality of the partnership-working. Good social work does not operate in isolation; the contributions of our key partners, schools, health and police are essential if we are truly to protect children well. Multi-agency audits are a key function delivered by local safeguarding children boards

(LSCBs). Knowing how our interventions are experienced by families is another critical part of understanding impact and what needs to improve, so reliable methods to secure feedback from children and their families and the commitment to act on that feedback are equally important.

We have spoken about the centrality of leadership and how it sets organisational culture. This is essentially about the professional leadership of the service. However, how it feels to be in the organisation is also influenced by the behaviour and contributions of others.

(b) Leadership of other corporate managers and political members

Children's social work is different from all other council-provided services, including, we suggest, adult social care. The levels of risk, exposure to pain, sadness, aggression, the potential for public humiliation – none of this is evident anywhere else in a local authority. Other public sector jobs are not easy, not least adult social care, but they are different and acknowledging that from the outset is a necessary condition for success. Chief executives and corporate managers need to find the line between recognition of these differences and the proper imposition of corporate identity and the corporate rules that all children's services should adhere to. Senior managers in children's services need to find the same meeting place. No matter how big or how busy the service, children's social care only ever deals with a very small proportion of the local community, so the relationship between the substantial and complex needs of the few always needs to be balanced with the needs and wishes of the whole.

Nowhere is this tension more readily or frequently played out than in the field of HR. HR is often where the dead hand of bureaucracy can be most powerfully felt, whether through the rigid imposition of a job evaluation scheme that simply cannot cope with the complexity of a social care manager's job (measuring numbers of staff or budgets held rather than risk carried) or in risk-averse advice designed to avoid at all costs a potential employment tribunal or … the list goes on – everyone will have their favourite HR 'computer says no' story. Sadly, few of us are able to describe circumstances where HR processes have been specifically designed to help us in the constant challenge of recruiting and retaining the best staff and in the delivery of our work. And it is processes that are nearly always the problem; we have worked with some exceptionally helpful HR staff.

The other key aspect of leadership is in the roles of team and first-line managers. These are crucial, sitting between the demands and pressures driven downwards from senior managers on the one hand and with direct responsibility for the management of cases and overseeing the quality of practice on the other. These staff are necessarily multiskilled and are nearly always the hardest level to recruit and retain. They need to have an eye on budget management, team functioning, applying HR procedures, seeing cases through their part of the system, bringing on new staff, keeping older staff motivated, responding to complaints and queries from senior managers, members, MPs – the list goes on. Increasingly, they are asked to do all this with ever-decreasing administrative support as they become more and more 'self-servicing', administering their own HR, budgets and performance systems online.

However, let us not forget that probably their most important role is that of supervisor. We ask social workers to go into some of the most difficult, traumatised, aggressive, sad, troubled families and ask them to build effective working relationships with those families and use those relationships to drive change for children. This entire chapter, in essence, sets out all that is required to make that task both do-able and effective. The provision of high-quality, insightful and reflective supervision is an absolute prerequisite for the task and as much effort and investment needs to go into building that capacity in an organisation as it does into practice development and practitioner training. Supervisors should be expected to regularly review the work of their staff in real circumstances through live observation and must be skilled at getting underneath cases and practitioners in order to offer genuine insights into both. The impact of the Munro review has, we think, been to increase the focus on supervision of staff and the quality of social work.

(c) Professional development

It goes without saying, or, again, at least it should, that enabling and expecting social workers to be good professionals is essential to any social care organisation. Sadly, not always so. The extent to which integrated computer systems (ICS) specifically, information technology (IT) systems generally and national micro-management have detracted from the profession has been well rehearsed and we will not echo that conversation here, save to say that the paper files predating ICS were all too often lacking any substance, as anyone who has taken a former care leaver from the 1950s, 1960s or 1970s through their files will know. Trying to show how and when decisions were made, when social workers visited them or their families, or how they did in school and finding not much more than internal administration forms and a bit of desultory casework recording is sad and distressing for worker and service user alike. So, the past was not always rose-coloured but recent history has not been helpful in the development of good social work practice in this country. Eileen Munro said it clearly but the overall response from the government to her recommendations in this respect has remained piecemeal and somewhat mealy-mouthed in our view.

Locally, however, there is scope to develop the profession. Some have taken this opportunity, and others, including some in our recent experience, have not. In too many instances we have seen the driving through of compliance and increased management grip adding to rather than offsetting a local authority's difficulties. In one (in)famous example, the form designed to capture the write-up of a social work visit had expanded to 19 pages, as more and more tick boxes had been added to meet the findings of an SCR or to capture latest research or governmental direction. And they wondered why social work engagement with families was not as required and why staff felt the grass would be greener elsewhere and left.

(d) Learning and development

Learning and development of staff is key. Too much training has, in our experience, become pedestrian and repetitive: the same increasingly tired programmes offered by the same trainers in the same 'classroom' style and often pitched at the 'lowest common denominator', with a remedial rather than a service-enhancement focus. Too much time has been wasted on these days and too many practitioners have not taken them seriously enough. This may just about work when what is required is the dissemination of new legislation or a significant policy change. It will not work when the task is about developing and enhancing skills in social work practice and linking knowledge to interventions. Action learning sets, practice educators on site, teams working together on new initiatives – there are a range of more effective ways of cracking this nut, almost any of which are proving more effective than previous methods.

Supervision, learning and development, and HR procedures and policies all come together when looking at professional and career development. If social work is truly to share the same characteristics of other professions (such as selectivity of entry and a select body of specialist knowledge), it must offer the equivalent possibility of career advancement and financial reward as other practising professionals. The very best lawyers, health consultants and head teachers continue to practise law, carry out operations or stand in front of classrooms as their careers develop and their salaries rise. The introduction of the principal social worker role, one of the recommendations arising from Munro's review, offers an opportunity for the same progression, but too often, these are one-off roles and in many authorities they are labels attached to an existing post. Something more comprehensive is required. Money spent on golden hellos or handcuffs would be better channelled into funding career development opportunities for our very ablest and skilled practitioners. This might mean having more flexible pay scales in local authorities and greater clarity about how we define 'good' (see earlier) but it is something that requires exploration.

All of us struggle with constant real or threatened overspends. We all work to try to reduce reliance on agency staff (where we think the sector has not punched with its full weight to drive down the excessive costs, but that is another chapter …) and to reduce numbers of children in residential care and independently fostered. It is increasingly clear, however, that the delivery of really good, professionally defined social work has as much positive impact on spend as better commissioning and contracting. Good social workers, enabled and expected to give of their best, deliver better and sharper assessments, and more focused and meaningful care plans, and children's journey through and out of the system is more timely and more effective. Good practice saves money. This means staff with caseloads that allow for quality intervention; caseload management is one of the key elements in any effective service. This is self-explanatory and needs little elaboration from us, save to say that piling too much work on too few staff in order to live within too small budgets can only end in tears. If nothing else more tragic occurs, what will happen is that staff will leave and reliance on agency staff will increase, with the associated costs.

The foregoing may read as if the responsibility for the delivery of good social work sits with the system, not with practitioners. What we hope is clearly implied (and in some organisations is set out very explicitly) is that if practitioners are to be both expected and enabled to do the difficult but necessary tasks that are the essence of social work, they have a right to expect the organisation where they work to deliver on its side of that deal, which is what this chapter has sought to set out.

Perhaps the recent direction from the Secretary of State to Doncaster Council to establish an independent trust to deliver children's social care will, as advertised, offer a genuine opportunity to see whether a different organisational arrangement – without the degree of political and corporate uncertainty that can negatively impact on the service in some authorities and support it in others – can work better. It is a challenging task for any authority to improve its service while undertaking such a major change as moving to a new organisation, especially for one already struggling to deliver improvements, so it may take time for this to really impact. However, it does offer the prospect of constructing a service 'fit for purpose' in all aspects from the very outset.

Finally, a word about sustainability. The detail of the work described earlier will vary across the country from one authority to another, and will find its expression in a number of different ways, but the underlying themes will be there and identifiable. Leaders and managers will come and go, politicians will come and go, and government imperatives will change year on year (at least), but the direction set by the successful implementation of this work is jeopardised at your peril. Of course, services need to change to take account of changing demand and legislation and nothing in what we set out should be imposed so rigidly that change becomes slow and laborious. Good services are light on their feet and able to adapt and bend as circumstances require. What should never be lost is the focus on organisational culture set out at the beginning of this chapter and the constant need to retain the humility with the confidence. Sustainability and the drive towards ever-improving outcomes are entirely dependent (in our view) on the sense that things are never good enough (and you know that because you look at the right things in the right way) and that the task of safeguarding children is so complex that it can never be said to be 'done'.

You do not need a weatherman to know which way the wind blows

Whatever an organisation's response to the detail of the Munro review, surely the single biggest contribution that the reforms have brought has been to articulate, eloquently and convincingly, what many in the sector have known for a long time: the task is complex; risks exist and cannot be managed away; adults harm children in circumstances that are not always predictable or preventable; and the system has been allowed to become unnecessarily and unhelpfully complicated.

Head teachers past and present, politicians, inspectors, consultants, and improvement partners all appear to mirror a belief that runs deep in society that running children's services is a straightforward matter, requiring little more than applied common sense and a modicum of intelligence and care and empathy for others (unless of course they are the monsters who should have their children removed at birth). Newspapers, especially in times of crisis, feed this view, and even post-Munro, the coverage is no more sophisticated or informed that it ever was, as an editorial in *The Times* showed immediately after the Pelka case (*The Times*, 2013). The belief seems to be that if only social care were staffed with those with an ounce or two of common sense, a little less concern with political correctness and the ability to see and react to the blindingly obvious, children would not die or be seriously injured in the way they repeatedly are. It is interesting that those head teachers and educationalists believe that no one save for another head teacher can understand or manage a school but they still approach the running of social care with a self-confidence and certainty that brook no argument. Of course, they all have something to offer and there are always things we can learn from others. What would be welcome would be a little less confidence and a little more humility.

Yes, of course we get it wrong sometimes, and this chapter is, we hope, something that will help in the avoidance of future errors and systemic failings, but, make no mistake, the expertise to run successful social care services is embedded in the sector – and pretty much else nowhere else.

References

Munro, E. (2011) *The Munro review of child protection. Final report: a child-centred system*, London: The Stationery Office.

Ofsted (Office for Standards in Education) (2013) *Framework and evaluation schedule for the inspection of services for children in need of help and protection, children looked after and care leavers (single inspection framework) and reviews of local safeguarding children boards*, Manchester: Ofsted.

The Times (2013) 'Editorial', 12 October.

2

Child protection: 40 years of learning but where next?

Ray Jones

The UK has had 40 years of learning about how to protect children from neglect and abuse. Based on the welfare state infrastructure built in the 1940s (Timmins, 1995), services, policies and practice have been developed incrementally to respond to and capture the learning. The consequence has been that when compared to other countries, the UK now has one of the lowest incidences of child deaths following the abuse and neglect of children, and this success has been stable and maintained for many years (Pritchard and Williams, 2009).

The journey over 40 years

It was 40 years ago in 1973 that there was a major public inquiry into the death of a seven-year-old girl from abuse (Department of Health and Social Security, 1974). Maria Colwell died in Brighton, having been neglected and abused in her family home and then violently assaulted by her stepfather. There had been other inquiries before, such as that into the death of Dennis O'Neill, a 14-year-old boy killed by his foster-father (Home Office, 1945), but what was new in 1973 was the media attention given to the Maria Colwell inquiry. In particular, anger about Maria's awful life and death was turned from the perpetrators of her neglect and abuse and directed at one of the professionals, Diana Lees, Maria's social worker, who sought to help families and to protect children. She was vilified in the press, described as 'the defendant' during the inquiry's proceedings, and harassed and threatened by a baying mob, who shouted at her during the hearings and chased her outside the inquiry, causing her to need police protection (Butler and Drakeford, 2011).

In addition to the Colwell inquiry being the first to attract such media attention, with hatred and harassment directed at the social worker, it was exceptional in that, alongside the majority inquiry report agreed by the barrister, doctor and councillor on the inquiry panel, a minority report was prepared by Olive Stevenson, the panel member who was a social worker. Stevenson died in 2013, 40 years after writing her minority report, and was a major contributor throughout her life to the improvement of child protection policy and practice. Her book on the neglect of children (Stevenson, 2007), for example, tackled concerns that where there was no apparent immediate danger or acute crisis, such as serious physical abuse and injury, decision-making for neglected children drifted, with all the damaging consequences for their welfare and development, a concern emphasised by Ward's research on poor parenting and infants (Ward, et al 2012).

In her minority report, Stevenson spelt out some of the realities for social workers working with families and seeking, when necessary, to protect children:

> there are few, if any situations of the kind in which Maria was involved which are 'black and white'. The harsh lesson which social workers in child care services have to learn is that ... there are very few situations in which choices are clear cut and predictable. (Department of Health and Social Security, 1974)

It was the Colwell inquiry, prompted no doubt by the resulting press and public interest and concern, which led to national guidance on how workers in different agencies should contribute and communicate to protect children. Since 1974 there have been other deaths of children that have attracted considerable media interest, further inquiries that have delved in detail into the work of agencies and professionals, and more and more guidance and proceduralisation, as central government uses these as levers to seek to drive up practice standards and consistency (Parton, 2011).

The deaths of children, and the subsequent inquiries and media attention, have also been seen as drivers for legislative change. The

Colwell inquiry, for example, was seen to lead to greater focus on 'rescuing' children from neglecting or abusive parents and the promotion of adoption – rather like Mr Gove's drive on adoption starting in 2011 – with the Adoption Act 1976 and the Children Act 1975 concentrating on permanence for children living away from their families. And the death of seven-year-old Victoria Climbié and the subsequent inquiry led by Lord Laming (Laming, 2003) were seen to have been the catalyst for the Children Act 2004, which led in England (but not elsewhere in the UK) to the disaggregation of social services departments led mainly by social workers and to the advent of local authority children's services departments led largely by former directors of education.

But in child protection there has always been a swinging pendulum. Theories and fashions change in line with political dogma and public mood, which is itself often shaped by a press promoting particular ideologies. So, in the midst of the 1980s and Thatcherism, with its attacks on the state and the somewhat misquoted view of Mrs Thatcher that 'there is no such thing as society' (Young, 1989; McSmith, 2011), and the devaluing of the competence and contribution of public sector professionals, there was the inquiry by Lady Justice Butler-Sloss into what was seen as the over-identification by two paediatricians of child sexual abuse in Cleveland, where courts directed the removal of children from their families (Butler-Sloss, 1988). There was also what was found to be the misidentification of satanic and ritual sexual abuse of children in Orkney (Clyde, 1992). Both Cleveland and rather more remotely Orkney were seen to have informed the philosophy underpinning the Children Act 1989 that social workers and others should engage in more partnership-working with parents, with an emphasis on assisting them in their care of children.

The argument, however, that it was high-profile inquiries – Colwell, Cleveland, Climbié and others – that led to legislative change, whether in the direction of more or less intervention to protect children, has been challenged (Jones, 2009). In each example there were other processes already under way. These included: commissions reviewing adoption or family law; changes in government policy pre-dating the child protection inquiry, such as the late 1990s/early

2000s New Labour government's emphasis on 'joining up' services through youth offending teams and in Sure Start centres; and key champions, such as Sir Keith Joseph (Rutter and Madge, 1976) and Kellmer Pringle (1975) in the mid-1970s and the Minister of State for Children, Margaret Hodge, in the early 2000s, who, as leader of Islington Council in the late 1980s, had led the development of joined-up neighbourhood services.

So, while the history of the past 40 years in England is complex and not always consistent, it still reflects incremental change, which overall has led to greater success in protecting children. However, this is not recognised by a public who are selectively fed stories by the media, especially the right-wing tabloid press led by *The Sun* and the *Daily Mail*, which are apparently chosen randomly from the 50 to 70 child deaths from neglect or abuse each year in England. The public will not know that this incidence of child deaths is lower than elsewhere and they will not know about the successful work in protecting much larger numbers of children. What they are led to understand is that social workers, among all those who work with children and have key roles in child protection, have 'failed' yet again and should be the subject of blame.

With this as the historical background, what has been learnt about how best to protect children? How has this learning been enabled and led? And what is the context for embedding and acting on this learning to improve child protection given the political philosophy and policies of the Coalition government elected in 2010? One crucial aspect of this context relevant for child protection is that, as a consequence of devolution, there are now four child protection systems in operation across the UK. Scotland and Northern Ireland already had devolved powers in relation to social services and this is now also the case for Wales. While England has moved to an emphasis on markets, competition and the privatisation of services, shrinking the welfare state and public services, other countries have maintained a commitment to public services and integration across the services. The following account relates to England.

Within this account, one major theme will emerge. It is the tension between what the Coalition government terms 'public accountability' and its impact on learning and action and whether this accountability is a euphemism for blame, with all the consequences of harassment and hatred directed at child protection workers, so that they are deterred from taking on or staying in child protection roles, and a drive towards defensive practice.

Learning and embedding

What has been learnt over the years about what constitutes good child protection practice and how far is this embedded in, or undermined by, current policies and practice? There are recurrent themes that have been emphasised over and over again from the serious case reviews (SCRs) following the serious injury or death of children and young people following neglect and abuse.

First, the importance of building up the picture of what is happening in the life of a child is crucial to the assessment of their risk and vulnerability. It includes the requirement that workers across all professional groups, including those who identify themselves as working primarily with adults, such as mental health and drug and alcohol workers, stay focused on, see and listen to children. They need to cover all the 'i's – being intrigued, imaginative, inquisitive, investigative and interrogative – as they seek to understand the child's experience.

In building up the picture of the child's experience, they also need to deliver on the further 'i's: capturing intelligence and information, and sharing it with others so the collated information informs the triangulated picture of the child's life and experience. 'Failings' in communication and interprofessional and interagency information sharing is a common finding in SCRs and concerns about confidentiality and data protection are often presented as inhibitors to information sharing. The ground rule should be to share information when there is a need to know in building an understanding of the child's experience. There is also the difficulty of within-agency information sharing, and the building of histories and understandings, being hindered and disrupted, because agencies have constructed complex internal arrangements with numerous handovers of children between teams and workers and because cases move, for example, from duty teams to initial assessment, to comprehensive assessment, to children in need, to child protection, to looked after, to leaving care. But information also needs structure so that sense can be made of the pieces of the information jigsaw. Child protection case conferences have been developed over the years as a means of promoting and enabling information sharing, but the reality is still that it is only when there is focus and adequate time allocated to an SCR that a fuller picture is created. This is especially so with the creation of integrated chronologies which capture all the multiprofessional and interagency contact and activity with a child and family. This has led to the recommendation that all child protection case conferences and review meetings should have available an integrated chronology (Nicolas, 2013).

Second, beyond information generation and sharing is the necessary assessment and action planning. The significant limitation often found in SCRs is that this becomes focused on the adults rather than the children. In particular, it focuses on mothers, with little attention given to fathers and other men in the child's life. And one of the criticisms of the tools and methods of working with parents is that they come to concentrate on the needs and wishes of parents while children shrink to the margins of attention.

Third, there has been the recurrent theme of professionals being too optimistic about the capacity of parents and other carers to improve their parenting and care of children. This is especially so in relation to neglect that becomes chronic over time. Because there is no urgent or immediate trigger that promotes action, there is drift, which leads to children never being subject to child protection assessments and action or children remaining on, or being on–off–on–off, child protection plans for years rather than months. The implications of this drift, with continuing chronic neglect, on the development of infants and very young children has been highlighted by recent research (Ward et al, 2012), and the more positive outcomes from taking action for older children have also been noted (Wade et al, 2011; Farmer and Wijedasa, 2013).

So, we know what makes for good child protection. It includes workers who stay focused on the child while working with families and while assessing adults and seeking where appropriate to change their parenting and caring behaviours, never losing focus on the child;

where workers know, trust and respect each other locally and share information and communicate well, and where there is a willingness and decisiveness to act if children are being neglected or abused rather than allowing drift. This is facilitated across all workers and agencies by the process of reflective supervision that promotes clarity about assessments, is challenging of judgements, may require further information to be sought and is outcome-focused for children. It also is supportive of workers so they are not practising in isolation with all the burdens of stress and anxiety that result.

Good practice is facilitated by organisational cultures that are open, where change is managed well and is more likely to be about fine-tuning than frequent 'big bang' reorganisations, and where there is an emphasis on performance within a learning culture (Senge, 1997). There will be continuity of senior managers, who stay informed about and close to front-line practice (Social Services Inspectorate and Audit Commission, no date) and there is recognition of the pivotal role of front-line managers for the day-to-day promotion and quality assurance of good practice.

Good child protection practice also requires stability across practitioners. It requires workers who become increasingly competent and confident through experience. There is no quick fix for expertise built through experience. Child protection requires intellectual capacity and rigour to be able to draw together disparate and dispersed information and to be able to use it to inform complex assessments and judgements based on practice wisdom and the knowledge base of research. There is also the requirement of intelligence and intellect to be able to conceptualise and communicate well because part of the child protection task includes informing others, including court decision-makers, about what is happening in a child's life and the impact this is having on the child.

In addition, good child protection requires emotional intelligence. Inevitably, child protection is work that is usually contested. Parents and others will often have different views and intentions from those of workers focused on the welfare and safety of the child. For the children, and for some adults, their lives are full of emotional confusion and trauma. Social work is often deployed at times of crisis and change within people's lives, including points of relationship conflict and breakdown or changing life circumstances such as recently diagnosed or changing long-term health conditions or impairment. These are times of what have been called 'psychosocial transitions' (Murray Parkes, 2013) and personal turmoil, where others may need to bring space and time to assist with problem-solving and life planning. These are emotionally challenging and draining times for all involved, including workers, and emotional intelligence informing relationships is key to good practice. Social workers and others are tasked to challenge and confront behaviours while maintaining and retaining contact and communication with those they are confronting.

It is this continuity of presence and contact over time that is key to good child protection. It is important in building the picture of what a child's life is like, which is inadequately informed by different and changing workers taking unrelated snapshots. Continuity is also important in building trust with children and others so that information and experiences are shared. And it is important in ensuring that actions are followed through, so there is not a pattern of repeated but incomplete assessments leading to the assessment itself becoming the activity and outcome.

The positive realities of child protection today

How do child protection policies, services and practice measure up against the yardstick of what is now known to make for good practice? There are many positives that reflect the implementation and follow-through of the learning of the past 40 years.

First, practice is more likely to be authoritative in its intention and goals. In the 1970s and 1980s it was not unusual for practice to be characterised as 'social work support'. This could mean being unfocused, unclear and uncertain about activity, intention and goals. Practice today, with the use of explicit assessments, case plans and contracts with parents and carers, and with monitoring and reviews in supervision as well as in multiple professional meetings, is more likely to be focused and outcome-oriented, with more challenge to parents and others.

Second, practice is more likely to be evidence-informed, with more known and knowledge more available about the efficacy of differing methods and models of work, about parenting styles and how these might be modified, and about the experiences and impact of these experiences on the welfare and development of children. It was only in the late 1960s into the 1970s that there was increasing awareness of the physical abuse of children; the 1980s into the 1990s saw an increasing awareness of the sexual abuse of children within families and in institutions; the 2000s saw increasing concern about the pervasive impact of chronic continuing neglect on children; and very recently new attention has been given to the networked sexual grooming and abuse of children. So, we know more and we are aware of more.

Third, there has been the creation and increasing availability of resources to assist families getting into difficulty, to work with parents and carers to improve parenting, and to be more available to children to hear about their experiences. From the advent of family centres in the 1980s, through Sure Start programmes in the early 2000s, evidence-informed parenting programmes, listening, advice and advocacy services for children such as ChildLine, and specialist services for children and young people who have run away or been sexually exploited and abused, the range of services and resources has increased over the years.

Fourth, although often experienced as much as a hindrance as a help, the development of policies and procedures to inform and unify practice has had the benefit of coding and promoting information sharing, well-structured and shaped assessments, and necessary practice activities, such as ensuring that children are seen and spoken to alone.

So, there is much in child protection to recognise as good and successful, and indeed as enhancements and improvements on what has gone before.

The problems today

It is increasingly difficult to practise child protection well. In part, this is about capacity. Good practice requires workers to spend time with children and families, building relationships and getting a strong view of the child's experience. Communication between workers and across agency boundaries also requires time and, when rushed, making a telephone call, sending an email or meeting and conversing together can get squeezed out when there are other more urgent and demanding actions to be taken across the whole caseload and workload. Being considered in making judgements and workers and supervisors protecting space for reflection can also be overwhelmed by the busyness of child protection front-line demands.

This has become worse and more difficult over the past five years. It is often referred to as the 'Baby P effect'. Seventeen-month-old Peter Connelly, known as 'Baby P' in press reports, died in August 2007 following neglect and horrific abuse. In November 2008, when his mother and two men were found guilty of causing or allowing his death, a media campaign began demanding the sacking of social workers, their managers and a paediatrician (Warner, 2013a, 2013b; Jones, 2014). Within weeks, there was a surge in care proceedings in the family courts, with new applications to courts increasing from 482 in October 2008 to 716 in December 2008, a 49% increase (CAFCASS, 2009, 2012), reflecting defensive but also more determined decision-making in child protection services.

On a range of measures, child protection workloads have increased since 2008 and 2009:

- Children-in-need new referrals to children's social services increased by 4.6%, from 377,600 in 2009/10 to 395,000 in 2011/12 (Department for Education, 2013a).
- Children Act 1989, section 47 child protection investigations increased by 42%, from 89,300 in 2009/10 to 127,000 in 2012/13 (Department for Education, 2013a).
- The number of children with child protection plans increased by 48%, from 29,200 on 31 March 2008 to 43,100 on the same date in 2013 (Department for Education, 2013a).
- Care proceedings increased by 71%, from 6,488 in 2008/09 to 11,101 in 2012/13 (CAFCASS, 2013).
- The number of children looked after in the care of local authorities increased by 12%, from 60,900 on 31 March 2009 to 68,100 on the

same date in 2013, with 62% of children looked after because they had been abused or neglected (Department for Education, 2013b).

Workloads have increased across the children's social care system but increases are especially extreme for child protection activity. This will have had an impact on all workers and agencies involved in child protection, with child protection investigations having increased by 42%, numbers of child protection plans by 48% and care proceedings by 71%.

Undertaking child protection investigations and assessments, creating and delivering child protection plans, with more case conferences, core group and review meetings, and preparing and presenting complex reports and evidence for care proceedings to hit the 26-week public law target for completion of proceedings are all especially time-consuming and onerous for social workers and for specialist police officers, health workers and lawyers working in child protection services.

The increase in child protection activity is not only a continuation and legacy, five years on, of the 'Baby P effect'. It also reflects a number of other changes over the past five years. For example, greater awareness of the impact of neglect and emotional abuse on children has led to an increase between 2008 and 2012 of 36% in the number of children with child protection plans where the primary concern has been neglect, with a 56% increase in the same period in child protection plans for children where emotional abuse has been the main concern.

Second, more families are probably getting into difficulty, with parents more stressed, harassed and exhausted, because of significant reductions in welfare and housing benefits (Higgs, 2012). Charitable food banks, even 'baby banks', increasingly offer the uncertain and tenuous means of providing food and clothing for children and adults who in the past may have experienced deprivation but who now are in the midst of destitution, something that Mr Gove, Secretary of State for Children, does not think should be of concern for social workers working with children and families (Randeep, 2013).

Third, assistance for families getting into difficulty, where parents may need help to parent well, is being cut, with funding for Sure

Start and children's centres significantly reduced and services closing (McCardle, 2013). This is of particular significance for those working in child protection, as the resources they can call on to assist families and monitor and improve the care of children are withdrawn or more heavily targeted. Families have to be in considerable difficulty, often at the point of decisions being made as to whether to seek the removal of children from families, before help is provided.

So, there is increasing need with less help to respond to that need and, with this, an increase in child protection referrals and activity but no commensurate increase in capacity to respond to increasing demand, as local councils and other public services have their funding reduced by the government (Donovan, 2013; Murray, 2013). This is all made even more difficult by three further factors, each of which is related to national politics and policy.

First, there is an emphasis, generated and required by national government, on reducing, breaking up and fragmenting public services and rolling back the welfare state. Across the public sector, the political intention of the current Conservative and Liberal Democrat Coalition government is to open up more and more services to the marketplace, with an emphasis on profit rather than public service and on competition rather than cooperation and collaboration. This has a particular impact on child protection. Good child protection, as noted earlier, requires workers and agencies working with and for children, and with the adults parenting those children, to communicate and collaborate well and it needs stability and continuity within and across services. It is also important that workers are embedded locally, so they have knowledge of families and of the networks and communities in which those families are engaged. But none of this may be a priority when the ownership of these new businesses lies with profit-driven and asset-stripping venture capitalists that may be based in the US, Europe or South East Asia. Even in the UK, the track record of companies such as Serco and G4S in the delivery of quality and value-for-public-money services has hardly been a beacon of excellence and probity.

And now there are schools as academies and free schools being set up in competition with each other, with the emphasis overwhelmingly on academic league tables. They have no requirement set by the government that they be partners with and within local child protection networks and systems. The community of schools in a local area has fragmented and local authorities are disempowered in trying to engage, co-ordinate and plan across what was the local education community. Yet councils and directors of children's services are misleadingly presented by government ministers as having the responsibility and leverage to tackle issues, including child protection issues, arising in schools (Harrington, 2013; Lock, 2013). There are particular concerns about schools now run by expanding national commercial companies, with an increasing number of academies within their management, where they are not engaging with local safeguarding children boards (LSCBs) and have isolated themselves.

The same trends and political and policy intentions, leading to fragmentation and competition overriding cooperation, can be seen across health, prison and soon probation services, all central to the provision of good child protection practice locally. And the consequence of cuts in policing and other public sector budgets is a move towards centralising services as a means of making savings, undermining local knowledge and local joint services and multi-agency working. It does not, of course, have to be like this, with some areas using the requirement to make savings to promote sharing of premises and management, but too often the easier quick fix when there is an urgency to make cuts fast is to reduce and retreat.

There is also an increasing denigration of public services by politicians, with a focus on health service and hospital failings and poor performance, and denigration also increasing for the police and schools and especially for local government services. Government ministers cut funding for services but then criticise those running the services when services have to be more heavily rationed and reduced.

For those working in child protection services, this is particularly pronounced and there is a particular mechanism in child protection for driving this process of denigration. SCRs were previously presented as primarily being about learning and improvement. They are now described on the Department for Education website as being about learning and allocating *accountability* (Department for Education, 2013c). Accountability itself is, in essence, not about taking responsibility to ensure that concerns are addressed and necessary improvements are made. Instead, it is about the allocation of responsibility, with accountability equated with blame when something terrible happens, even if it was not reasonably predictable from what was known at the time. This quote is from a *Mail on Sunday* editorial following the judgment by the Court of Appeal that Sharon Shoesmith, Haringey's Director of Children's Services at the time Peter Connelly died, had been scapegoated:

> Blame is not just a game, Ms Shoesmith …where life and death are concerned, especially the lives and deaths of helpless children, there must always be blame and there must always be people who are prepared, in the end, to accept it. (*Mail on Sunday*, 2011)

The *Mail on Sunday*'s statement that someone should be blamed for Peter Connelly's terrible death is not about blaming the perpetrators who caused or allowed him to die so horrifically. Instead, the blame must be allocated to and accepted by those who give their professional lives to protecting children. It is a frightening and fearful scenario for all who work in child protection.

SCRs feed and fuel this allocation of blame. The government now requires that they are published in full and has set up an 'expert panel' to oversee and promote their publication. The panel has four members: a journalist, an air accident investigator, a barrister and a former Department for Education (DfE) civil servant who is now the chief executive of the National Society for the Prevention of Cruelty to Children (NSPCC) (HM Government, 2013a). None has any experience of front-line child protection.

SCRs have also become a part of the child protection problem (Jones, 2013a; Kearney, 2013). They are costly in terms of time and cash and distract managers from the current management of services as they are focused on retrospective analysis. The SCR process has focused on drilling down in considerable detail on one case, with all the benefit of hindsight knowing that something awful has happened, with little or no consideration of the wider workload and organisational context for the workers concerned and with the workers themselves marginalised and excluded throughout the SCR process, which itself concentrates on a description of what happened rather than informed analysis. Judgements made in the SCR process are often based on ideal rather than practicable standards and their output is usually a large number of – 40 plus – recommendations (Sidebotham, 2013), many focused on introducing more policies and procedures when organisations are already constipated by the numerous policies and procedures introduced and poorly implemented from previous SCRs.

It is likely that with 150 to 200 SCRs completed a year, there have been more than 4,000 SCRs completed over the past 20 years. It is not surprising therefore that SCRs rarely generate any new learning. What they do generate is the ammunition for politicians, press and public to allocate blame to workers and at an annual cost in cash and cash-costed time of about £9 million based on 150 reviews at £60,000 per review. In addition, there has been the increasingly used process of the Minister for Children publicly criticising and undermining individual SCRs when they become high-profile (Hayes, 2013) and with seeking accountability and responsibility and allocating blame, as with the Daniel Pelka/Coventry SCR (Lock, 2013) and the Hamzah Khan/Bradford report (BBC, 2013). It has been reported that the public vilification of social workers is causing difficulties in recruiting and retaining children's services social workers (Holmes et al, 2013; Horton, 2013; *Reading Post,* 2013).

But it is not only SCRs that have become a process for allocating accountability and blame. Office for Standards in Education (Ofsted) inspections of child protection services have become more demanding, with more stringent standards set and grading categories labelled more negatively. This is at a time when child protection services across the country are under more pressure and less likely to be able to achieve and sustain the more rigorous Ofsted standards and with inspectorial scrutiny itself a time-consuming burden for local services.

In its 2013 report of social care, Ofsted itself noted:

> The past decade has seen a series of high profile inquiries and reviews following the deaths or serious injuries of children. This has triggered a major programme of

reform, some of which is only now beginning to take shape. There is greater public awareness of abuse and neglect in families and, being at the forefront of this concern, local authorities are managing increasing workloads. This comes at a time when expenditure in the public sector is decreasing. These factors create a pressurised environment that magnifies the impact of weaknesses in some local authority areas....

Data from the Institute for Fiscal Studies on central government funding allocation to local government show a 26.6% reduction in local authority budgets in the five years from 2010. Meanwhile, it has been reported that, although some areas have invested in more frontline social work posts, the number of children's social care posts across the UK has fallen by 4%. Inspection evidence from local authorities and children's homes shows the disruptive impact of using short-term staffing solutions, particularly when the annual staff turnover rate of care staff can be as high as 16%. (Ofsted, 2013, pp 6, 8)

The consequences for the increasing number of local areas and councils judged 'inadequate' by the enhanced Ofsted standards are that, not surprisingly, they find it more difficult to retain and recruit workers, becoming dependent on expensive but short-term agency and interim practitioners and managers, which undermines the stability and continuity needed for good child protection practice. They have a workforce that becomes skewed towards newly qualified, less experienced workers, where there is often a change in top managers, with a third of directors of children's services changing in a year:

In this context, we are concerned about reports that, in the past year, 32% of local authorities saw at least one change in the post holder of director of children's services in the course of the year, with some local authorities seeing multiple changes in the post holder in a single year.

> A persistent absence of stable leadership was a feature of most inadequate local authorities. Changes in leadership as a response to poor performance made sustainable improvement difficult, hampering action to address serious system and practice failures. (Ofsted, 2013, p 20)

Following an 'inadequate' Ofsted judgement, referrals to child protection processes increase locally as all workers and agencies lose confidence in assessing and triaging risk. It is, at least for a time until confidence and management grip is established, the doomsday scenario of an unstable workforce overloaded with more work and with no consistent leadership.

The route ahead

This chapter started with a glass half-full story of improvements over the past 40 years in child protection policies and practice. The picture subsequently painted of the context and realities of child protection today is less rosy. The data show that there are significant pressures on and within child protection services, that these have increased over the past five years, and that the organisational context for child protection services has become more fragmented. So, what lies ahead?

There are considerable dangers looming large for child protection. Many of the concerns are continuations and intensifications of the issues noted earlier, which are impinging on child protection. More families and children will become poorer, with deprivation replaced by destitution as the Coalition government continues with its austerity agenda. There is a political intention to cut welfare benefits further. More families in trouble means more work for those who provide assistance to families and protection for children.

But the next four to five years are planned to be a time of further cuts to public service budgets, so the capacity to assist the greater number of families in difficulty will inevitably be reduced. And while budgets are being cut and services closed, there will also be the disruption of organisational and governance changes across the National Health Service (NHS), schools, probation, the police and other services.

The ownership of these services will also change, with more services opened up to competitive tendering, so that companies such as Virgin Care, Serco (Syal, 2013), G4S, Capita and other less well-known companies, including iMPOWER and Cambridge Education, enter the marketplace in child protection. Many of the larger companies are internationally controlled and led, venture capital-funded businesses focused on profit margins. Mr Gove has been explicit that his agenda is that children's social care services should operate within this brave new commercial and fragmented world (HM Government, 2013b; Richardson, 2013).

How is this to be achieved for child protection? First, independent social work practices are being promoted, although there is little evidence of them improving outcomes for children (Stanley et al, 2012). These might have some attraction for social workers who want to escape working in large bureaucracies, with the setting up of non-profit-making social enterprises and public interest companies. But social work practices will not have to be led by social workers and indeed may not have to employ registered social workers. This may be a Trojan Horse, opening up social work services to the marketplace (Puffett, 2013b). If such companies are found to be potentially profitable, it is likely they will be aggregated up and integrated into bigger commercial organisations. It is happening already with academy schools. They may also be lightly regulated (Puffett, 2013c).

Second, as more local authorities struggle to deliver child protection services that meet the more stringent Ofsted standards at a time of funding cuts and increasing local need generating greater workloads, the government is already preparing the ground and positioning itself to remove child protection responsibilities from local councils and pass them to independent companies. Doncaster and Birmingham have already faced this scenario.

Third, SCRs may become even more of a tool for allocating blame and may become more of a centrally controlled expanding business enterprise. There are possible developments being considered for government funding of the Social Care Institute for Excellence and the NSPCC to control the training of independent SCR report authors and to determine who can be appointed to prepare SCR reports, with central moderation and approval of the reports before publication (Bichard, 2013). This would undermine LSCBs and their independent chairs. They are already having to account for their SCR decisions to the national SCR panel set up by government and they are now to be inspected by Ofsted. They may also find that their scope to appoint independent SCR panel chairs and overview report authors will be constrained and determined by government-funded national organisations.

So, there are understandable concerns that child protection practice in England may be undermined by cuts and fragmentation resulting from political dogma, with practitioners and managers being caught in an escalating culture of blame. There are, however, some positive developments for SCRs. In Wales, SCRs are triaged and applied more proportionately, with the full SCR process not always required. In England, a systems model has been piloted (Munro and Hubbard, 2011), which is much more participative for practitioners. It also focuses on understanding how and why decisions and actions took place given what was known at the time, considers context as much as case, and is concentrated on learning rather than allocating accountability and blame. How this will be allowed within a government requirement that SCR reports are published in full, despite this breaching confidentiality for families and others, and the allocation of accountability now central to every SCR, deterring practitioners from open engagement in the SCR process, is uncertain. When used in full, the systems approach is also at least as time-consuming as the traditional model of independent management reviews, which are prepared separately by each agency and then contribute to an independently prepared overview report.

When there is no requirement to do an SCR, LSCBs have been using the opportunity to carry out management reviews. For example, Salford LSCB undertook a multi-agency management review with an independently prepared integrated chronology based on contributions from each agency. The integrated chronology was presented to and discussed at a meeting of all practitioners and managers in a morning workshop and all were involved in developing an action plan to implement learning in the afternoon. This process can be accomplished in weeks rather than months.

There is, however, the danger of social workers in child protection becoming technicians rather than professionals. The fast-track Frontline social work training (Frontline, 2013) funded by central government may draw a few more bright graduates into social work. But they will be exposed very early in their social work practice careers (which will be short and curtailed as, even if they stay in work related to social work, they are intended to be fast-tracked to management) to sharp-end, difficult and distressing child protection decision-making with considerable exposure before they have had time to build confidence and competence based on experience and practice wisdom (McGregor, 2013). They are also being trained as specialists dealing with child protection.

This narrowing of social work was rejected by the Social Work Task Force (2010). It argued that specialisation should be focused on post-qualifying education and that taking on child protection lead responsibilities was a role and task for social workers with two years' plus experience. This is being reshaped and largely redefined, and is reinforced by recommendations in the Narey review of social work education (Department for Education, 2014) commissioned by the Secretary of State for Children. Specialisation and exposure too early will leave inexperienced workers, and the agencies employing them, very vulnerable.

There are, however, improvements that could be made to social work education. In particular, more needs to be done to bridge and break down the divide between higher education and social work agencies. The current arrangement of students spending time in the education institution and time on placement in practice agencies largely leaves the student having to translate learning into practice. More social work educators should continue for some of their time in practice so their practical experience is up to date. There should also be more continuous learning for practice educators in social work agencies so they are up to date with research. And social work agencies should seek social work teaching agency status, with the reinvention of student units, so that the time students spend on placement is a larger part of the qualifying degree programme. All of this might be assisted by higher education institutions and practice agencies making more joint appointments. Finally, a nationally required post-qualifying structure for social workers should be established and mandatory.

There are also other positive possibilities. The Social Work Task Force (2010) recommended that an independent college of social work be established to promote and enhance social work and that a chief social worker be appointed to advise government. At this time, The College of Social Work (TCSW) is dependent on government funding and, rather than having one chief social worker, the government has appointed a chief social worker for children based in the Department for Education and, separately, a chief social worker for adults in the Department of Health. This may reflect an increasing fragmentation of the social work profession as it comes to be defined even more by government-defined tasks allocated to social workers based on departmental divisions in Whitehall.

The Munro review of child protection (2011a, 2011b) canvassed for more space to be opened up for professional social work practice and a rebalancing of activity away from over-proceduralisation and hitting data-defined performance timescales and targets. The review and revision of *Working together* has resulted in much shorter national statutory guidance, and the reduction of national performance targets allows for more local discretion in how services are monitored and measured. But the likelihood, amidst more work to be done and no commensurate increase in resources and capacity, is that corners will be cut and cases closed down quickly to allow new work to be taken on. The ambition of Munro that practitioners should spend more time with children and families is not likely to be achieved in the current workload context.

Munro also sought a move away from crisis work focused on child protection to early intervention and family support. This, too, is an ambition challenged by increasing child protection workloads and the government cutting and abandoning its earmarked funding for Sure Start and other early years and early intervention programmes (Puffett, 2013a). Many local authorities are responding to significant budget reductions by shrinking youth services and heavily targeting the family and youth services that remain on those who are already in considerable difficulty.

—

The new models for organising practice may offer positive opportunities to promote space for working with families. The 'reclaiming social work' model, developed in Hackney in part by the chief social worker for children (Goodman and Trowler, 2011) and praised by Professor Munro (Garboden, 2010), had the promise of promoting the role of social workers but its wider rollout has been hampered and undermined by increasing child protection workloads overwhelming small social work units and by the focus on systemic therapeutic work with families, which is also central to the Frontline training of social workers, concentrating attention on adults and losing the focus on children (Cooper, 2013; Jones, 2013b).

Possibly, however, it is the models of intensive multiprofessional and multi-agency practice targeted on 'troubled families' (Department for Communities and Local Government, 2012) that offer a way forward. The national 'troubled families' programme was initially viewed suspiciously and sceptically by many as being about social control and penalising families in difficulty (Gregg, 2010; Levitas, 2012). But the relationship-based and practically oriented practice that has been developed has led to exhausted parents, often single-parent mothers, overwhelmed by poverty and debt, overcrowded and poor housing and physical and mental ill health, with little energy or time left for parenting, to share their concerns with 'troubled families' workers. They are helping them get some structure and shape back in their lives, and providing advocacy and assistance to mitigate the demands and threats experienced from others, including from a range of state agencies (Thoburn et al, 2013; Jones, 2013c; Jones, 2013d; Jones et al, forthcoming).

So, it seems that child protection is at a crucial cusp. Current difficulties and pressures may be used by government to legitimise the increasing privatisation of child protection services. If so, the longer-term consequences may be fragmentation, competition and the hunt for profit overriding coherence, collaboration and a focus on delivering a safe service for children.

Alternatively, there is a time-limited moment when the narrative might be changed from accountability being synonymous with blame and instead related to the requirement that child protection is adequately resourced, that families getting into difficulty receive assistance, that the punitive and penalising policies making good parenting more difficult for poor families are abandoned, and that child protection workers across all professions and agencies are given public support and recognition. It is an argument that needs to be won.

References

BBC (2013) 'Hamzah Khan: minister attacks starved boys findings', 13 November. Available at: www.bbc.co.uk/nesws/uk-england-29425704

Bichard, Lord (2013) 'A three-point child protection plan', *Local Government Chronical*, 7 November.

Butler, I. and Drakeford, M. (2011) *Social work on trial: the Colwell inquiry and the state of welfare*, Bristol: Policy Press.

Butler-Sloss, E. (1988) *Report of the inquiry into child abuse in Cleveland 1987*, Cm 412, London: HMSO.

CAFCASS (Children and Family Court Advisory and Support Service) (2009) 'CAFCASS care demand', press release, 8 May, London: CAFCASS.

CAFCASS (2012) *Three weeks in November ... three years on ...,* Care application study, London: CAFCASS.

CAFCASS (2013) 'Care applications in November 2013'. Available at: www.cafcass.gov.uk/news/2013/december/november-2013-care-demand-statistics.aspx

Clyde, Lord (1992) *The report of the inquiry into the removal of children from Orkney in February 1991: return to an address of the Honourable the House of Commons*, Norwich: The Stationery Office.

Cooper, J. (2013) 'Stress-busting Hackney model under threat from cherry picking councils', *Community Care*, 16 July. Available at: http://communitcare.co.uk/2013/07/16/stress-bsutonyg-hackney-model-uner-threat-from-cherry-picking-councils

Department for Communities and Local Government (2012) *The Troubled Families programme*, London: DCLG. Available at: www.communities.gov.uk/communities/troubledfamilies

Department for Education (2013a) *Characteristics of children in need, 2012–2013*, London: DfE. Available at: www.gov.uk/government/publications/characteristics-of-children-in-need-in-england-2012-to-2013

Department for Education (2013b) *Children looked after in England, including adoption*, London: DfE. Available at: www.gov.uk/government/publications/children-looked-after-in-england-including-adoption

Department for Education (2013c) *Serious case reviews*, London: DfE. Available at: www.education.gov.uk/childrenandyoungpeople/safeguardingchildren/reviews/a0068869/scrs

Department for Education (2014) *Making the education of social workers consistently effective: Report of Sir Martin Narey's independent review of the education of children's social workers*, London: DfE.

Department of Health and Social Security (1974) *Report of the inquiry into the care and supervision provided in relation to Maria Colwell*, London: DHSS/HMSO, p45.

Donovan, T. (2013) 'Protection for adults but cuts for children: how Osborne's plans affect social care', *Community Care*, 28 June. Available at: www.communitycare.co.uk/2013/06/28/protection-for-adults-but-cuts-for-childrens-social-care

Farmer, E. and Wijedasa, D. (2013) 'The reunification of looked after children with their parents: what contributes to return stability?', *British Journal of Social Work*, 43(8), 1611–29.

Frontline (2013) 'Changing lives'. Available at: www.thefrontline.org.uk

Garboden, M. (2010) 'Munro plaudit for Hackney's Reclaim Social Work model', *Community Care*, 17 December. Available at: www.communitycare.co.uk/2010/12/17/munro-plaudit-for-hackneys-reclaim-social-work-model

Goodman, S. and Trowler, I. (eds) (2011) *Social work reclaimed: innovative frameworks for child and family social work practice*, London: Jessica Kingsley Publishers.

Gregg, D. (2010) *Family intervention projects: a classic case of policy-based evidence*, London: Centre for Crime and Justice Studies. Available at: www.crimeandjustice.org.uk

Harrington, K. (2013) *Child G: a serious case review*, 16 December, East Sussex LSCB. Available at: www.eastsussexlscb.org.uk/user_controlled_lcms_area/uploaded_files/SCR%20Child%20G%20December%202013%20PUBLISHED.pdf

Hayes, D. (2013) 'Daniel Pelka: children's minister questions methods used in review', 17 September. Available at: www.cypnow.co.uk/cyp/news/1078388/childrens-minister-questions-scr-methods-pelka-review

Higgs, L. (2012) '"Terrifying" welfare reforms will drive up care referrals, warns Munro', *Children and Young People Now*, 6 July. Available at: www.cypnow.co.uk/print_article/cyp/news/1073834/munro-warns-welafre-policy-drive-referrals-social-care-services

HM Government (2013a) 'Serious review panel established', press release, 6 June, London: DfE. Available at: www.gov.uk/government/news/serious-case-review-panel-established

HM Government (2013b) 'Getting it right for children in need', Michael Gove speech to NSPCC, 12 November. Available at: www.gov.uk/government/speeches/getting-it-right-for-children-in-need-speech-to-the-nspcc

Holmes, E., Miscampbell, G. and Robin, B. (2013) *Reforming social work: improving social worker recruitment and retention*, London: Policy Exchange.

Home Office (1945) *Report by Sir William Monckton KCMG KCVO MC KC on the circumstances which led to the boarding out of Dennis and Terence O'Neill at Bank Farm, Minsterly and the steps taken to supervise their welfare, etc,* Cmd 6636, London: Home Office.

Horton, C. (2013) 'Name-and-shame culture is driving child protection professionals out of the sector', *Guardian*, 16 October. Available at: www.theguardian.com/social-care-newtork/2013/oct/16/name-and-shame-culture-is-driving-child-protection-professionals-out-of-the-sector

Jones, R. (2009) 'Children's Acts 1948–2008: the drivers for legislative change of 60 years', *Journal of Children's Services*, 4(1), 39–52.

Jones, R. (2013a) 'Child protection: serious case reviews feed the blame culture', *Guardian*, 8 October. Available at: theguardian.com/social-care-network/2013/oct/08/serious-case-reviews-feed-the-blame-culture.

Jones, R. (2013b) 'I am now anxious about how the Hackney model is being interpreted and rolled out', *Community Care*, 24 October. Available at: http://communitcare.co.uk/2013/10/24/i-am-anxious-about-how-the-hackney-model-is-being-interpreted-and-rolled-out.

Jones, R. (2013c) 'Baby P legacy five years on: what has been the impact in child protection', *Guardian,* 11 November. Available at: www.the guardian.com/social-care-network/2013.no/11/baby-p-legacy-impact-on-child-proteection.

Jones, R. (2013d) 'How to privatise child protection in easy stages', *Guardian*, 19 November. Available at: www.theguardian.com/society/2013/nov/nov/19/privatise-child-protection-michael-gove-social-workers.

Jones, R. (2014) *The 'story of Baby P': setting the record straight*, Bristol: Policy Press.

Jones, R., Matczak, A., Davis, K. and Byford, I. (forthcoming) *'Troubled families': a team around the family*.

Kearney, J. (2013) 'Something seriously wrong with SCRs', *Professional Social Work*, December, pp 26–27.

Kellmer Pringle, M. (1975) *The needs of children*, London: Hutchinson.

Laming, Lord (2003) *Victoria Climbié inquiry*, Cm 5730, Norwich: The Stationery Office.

Levitas, R. (2012) 'There may be "trouble" ahead: what we know of those 120,000 "troubled' families"', *Poverty and Social Exclusion*. Available at: www.poverty.ac.uk

Lock, R. (2013) *Serious case review re: Daniel Pelka*, Coventry LSCB, September. Available at: www.coventrylscb.org.uk/files/SCR/FINAL%20Overview%20Report%20%20DP%20130913%20Publication%20version.pdf

Mail on Sunday (2011) 'Blame is not just a game, Ms Shoesmith', 29 May, p 27.

McCardle, L. (2013) 'Children's centres serve more families as budgets are squeezed', *Children and Young People Now*, 29 October. Available at: www.cypnow.co.uk/print_article/cyp/news/1139641/childrens-centres-serve-familes-budgets-squeezed

McGregor, K. (2013) 'Can you teach social work students professional confidence in one year?', *Community Care*, 19 August. Available at: www.communitycare.co.uk/blogs/social-work-blog/2013/08/can-you-teach-social-work-students-professional-confidence-in-one-year

McSmith, A. (2011) *No such thing as society: a history of Britain in the 1980s*, London: Constable.

Munro, E. (2011a) *The Munro review of child protection. Interim report: the child's journey*, London: DfE.

Munro, E. (2011b) *The Munro review of child protection. Final report: a child-centred system*, Cm 8062, Norwich: The Stationery Office.

Munro, E. and Hubbard, A. (2011) 'A systems approach to evaluating organisational change in children's social care', *British Journal of Social Work*, 41(4), 726–43.

Murray, K. (2013) 'Social care: under pressure like never before', *Guardian*, 16 October. Available at: www.theguardian.com/social/-care-newtork/2013/oct/16/social-care-under-ptressure-like-never-before

Murray Parkes, C. (2013) *Love and loss: the roots of grief and its complications*, London: Routledge.

Nicolas, J. (2013) 'Child protection: to assess risk, professionals need to know all the facts', *Guardian*, 29 October. Available at: www.theguardian.com/social-care-network/2013/oct/29/child-protection-assess-risk-professionals

Ofsted (Office for Standards in Education) (2013) *Social care annual report, 2012–2013*. Available at: www.ofsted.gov.uk/resources/social-care-annual-report-201213

Parton, N. (2011) *The increasing length and complexity of central government guidance about child abuse in England: 1974–2010*, discussion paper, Huddersfield: University of Huddersfield. Available at: http://eprints/hud/ac/uk/9006/

Pritchard, C. and Williams, R. (2009) 'Comparing possible "child-abuse-related-deaths" in England and Wales with the major developed countries, 1974–2006: signs of progress?', *British Journal of Social Work*, 40(6), 1700–18.

Puffett, N. (2013a) 'Councils predict sharp fall in early years spending', *Children and Young People Now*, 7 October. Available at: www.cypnow.co.uk/print_article/cyp/news/1119015/councils-predict-sharp-fall-spending

Puffett, N. (2013b) 'Independent provider plans could lead to "privatisation" of social work, warns experts', *Children and Young People Now*, 16 October. Available at: www.cypn0w.co.uk/ptint_article/cyp/news/1119158/independent-provider-plans-lead-privatisation-warns-experts

Puffett, N. (2013c) 'Tougher requirements for independent social work providers rejected', *Children and Young People Now*, 28 October. Available at: www.cypnow.co.uk/print-article/cyp/news/1139606/tougher-requirements-independent-social-providers-rejected

Randeep, R. (2013) 'Michael Gove on quest to reform social work training', *Guardian*, 12 November. Available at: www.theguardian.com/society/2013/nov/12/michael-gove-reform-social-work

Reading Post (2013) '"Vilification" blamed for social work vacancies in Reading', 10 October. Available at: www.getreading.co.uk/news/local-news/vilification-blamed-social-work-vacancies

Richardson, H. (2013) 'More child protection takeovers ahead, Gove hints', BBC, 12 November. Available at: www.bbc.co.uk/news/education-24904031

Rutter, M. and Madge, N. (1976) *Cycles of disadvantage*, London: Heinemann.

Sidebotham, P. (2013) 'Daniel Pelka: do serious case reviews work?', quoted in T. Jones, 17 September. Available at: www.bbc.co.uk/news/uk-england-24107377

Senge, P.M. (1997) 'The fifth discipline', *Measuring Business Excellence*, 1(3), 46–51.

Social Services Inspectorate and Audit Commission (no date) *People need people: realising the potential of people working in the social services*, Abingdon: Audit Commission.

Social Work Task Force (2010) *Building a safe and confident future: final report of the Social Work Task Force*, London: DfE.

Stanley, N., Austerberry, H., Bilson, A., Farrelly, N., Hargreaves, K., Hollingworth, K., Hussein, S., Ingold, A., Larkins, C., Manthorpe, J., Ridley, J. and Strange, V. (2012) *Social work practices: report of the national evaluation*, London: DfE. Available at: www.gov.uk/government/uploads/system/uploads/attachment_data/file/183309/DFE-RR233.pdf

Stevenson, O. (2007) *Neglected children and their families*, Oxford: Blackwell.

Syal, R. (2013) 'Social services for vulnerable children in England to be privatised: Serco may be among firms bidding for contracts as Labour show concern over removal of checks that safeguard standards', *Guardian*, 18 July. Available at: www.theguardian.com/society/2013/jul/18/social-services-children-privatised-labour

Thoburn, J., Cooper, N., Brandon, M. and Connelly, S. (2013) 'The place of "think family" approaches in child and family social work: messages from a process evaluation of an English pathfinder service', *Children and Youth Services Review*, 35, 228–36.

Timmins, N. (1995) *The five giant: a biography of the welfare state*, London: Fontana.

Wade, J., Biehal, N., Farrelly, N. and Sinclair, I. (2011) *Caring for abused and neglected children: making the right decisions for reunification or long-term care*, London: Jessica Kingsley Publishers.

Ward, H., Brown, R. and Westlake, D. (2012) *Safeguarding babies and very young children from abuse and neglect*, London: Jessica Kingsley Publishers.

Warner, J. (2013a) 'Social work, class politics and risk in the moral panic over Baby P', *Health, Risk and Society*, March. Available at: http://dx.doi.org/10.1080/13698575.2013.776018

Warner, J. (2013b) '"Heads must roll"? Emotional politics, the press and the death of Baby P', *British Journal of Social Work*. Available at: http://dx.doi.org/10.1093/bjsw/bct039

Young, H. (1989) *One of us: a biography of Margaret Thatcher*, London: Macmillan.

3

Doing something different: reconfiguring front-line services: opening up the market

Chris Wright

The open public services programme outlined by the Coalition government challenges the default position that public services should be delivered by government or other public bodies. It encourages choice and competition to improve the efficiency and quality of services for the public, meaning that new providers such as charities, public sector mutuals and private sector organisations will play a much greater role in the provision of public services (HM Government, 2011).

This agenda has been discussed mainly in terms of what it will mean for education, the National Health Service (NHS) and probation (HM Government, 2013). Less has been said about what it will mean for young people and family services post-Munro, although it is encouraging that the government has launched a children's services innovation programme which invites the most 'ingenious and dynamic ventures' to transform children's services (Timpson, 2013).

This chapter will explore what the reforms under way could mean for the design, commissioning and delivery of services for young people and families. Using the Munro principles as a framework, it examines how services could be designed differently, around the professional, to achieve better outcomes. It is written from the perspective of a social business with more than 200 years' experience of working with young people, which sees the wider reforms as an important opportunity to improve current children's services and free up professionals so they can focus on the needs of the service user, their families and carers.

The burning platform

There has been a substantial increase in the demand for children's social care. This is evident in the numbers of initial assessments undertaken by local authorities, section 47 inquiries, identified children in need and young people taken into the care of the state. Between 2011 and 2012, over 600,000 children in England were referred to local authority children's social care services and numbers of children in need stood at 369,400 (Knox, 2012).[1] The number of looked-after children has increased steadily each year and, at 68,110, is higher than at any time since 1985. The main reason for young people being provided with a service continues to be abuse or neglect (Glenndenning, 2013).

The rise in demand can be accounted for by more effective safeguarding processes, following a series of high-profile cases concerning the death or injury of children at the hands of their parents or carers, and the raised expectations arising from Secretary of State Michael Gove's view that more young children should be taken into care at an earlier stage.[2] Ultimately, it could be argued that this rise indicates that the current model of service provision is not preventing enough young people and families from getting to crisis point.

For those young people and families who do find themselves coming into contact with social services, the latest (2012/13) *Social care annual report* undertaken by the Office for Standards in Education (Ofsted) reveals a very mixed picture of service user experience and a system operating under great pressure (Ofsted, 2013). The consequence of model failure is borne by the young people and their families – and ultimately by the taxpayer. For those who enter the care system, care can make a difference, and does for some, but the impact is not positive enough. This is not to say that there are not examples of good practice in local authority provision – there are, and certain outcomes are improving. While we should always keep in

---

[1] See: www.gov.uk/government/uploads/system/uploads/attachment_data/file/219174/sfr27-2012v4.pdf

[2] Address by the Secretary of State for Education, Rt Hon Michael Gove MP, to the Durand Academy, 1 September 2011, London.

mind the challenging complexities of young people the care system is working with, in the main, the system continues to disadvantage young people as they make their transition from care to adulthood.

Children in care are over-represented in a range of vulnerable groups, including those not in education, employment or training (NEETs), teenage parents, young offenders and those with substance misuse problems:

- Despite a narrowing of the attainment gap, the percentage of looked-after children who achieve each GCSE outcome is much smaller than the percentage of non-looked-after children. At key stage 4, 15% achieved 'the basics': A*–C in GCSE English and mathematics (Glenndenning, 2013).
- The number of 19-year-olds who were looked after at age 16 and are now NEET is 34%, a decrease of 1% on the previous year but still nearly double the rate of their non-care contemporaries (Glenndenning, 2013).
- Less than 1% of all children in England are in care but looked-after children make up 30% of boys and 44% of girls in custody (Murray, 2012, cited in Prison Reform Trust, 2013).
- Children in care are three times more likely to run away, with an estimated 10,000 going missing every year (UK Missing Children's Bureau, 2012, cited in Prison Reform Trust, 2013).
- Around a quarter of those living on the street have a background in care (Crisis and CRESR, 2011, cited in Prison Reform Trust, 2013).
- Care leavers are four times more likely to commit suicide in adulthood (Department of Health, 2012).

Recent research and investigation by the Children's Commissioner (2012) has highlighted the disproportionate prevalence of sexual exploitation among young people in the care of local authorities. The Commissioner has estimated that, in one year, at least 16,500 children were at risk of sexual exploitation and 2,409 children were confirmed as victims of sexual exploitation in gangs and groups.

Outcomes such as these cost the taxpayer approximately £3 billion a year. The majority of expenditure in 2012 was spent on foster care services and residential services (Ross, 2012).[3] The government's troubled families programme identified that eight times more money is spent on reacting to the problems of troubled families – which contain children in need – than on delivering targeted interventions to turn around their lives (Department for Communities and Local Government, 2013). The programme also identified evidence of duplication, with multiple agencies delivering similar interventions to the same families. The relational and collaborative approach adopted by the troubled families agenda could be viewed as a metaphor for what is needed for wider system change, emphasising the benefits of strong relationships acting as a single point of contact and the importance of working well in partnership with others.

The rising numbers of young people in need and taken into the care of the state, the costs, and poor outcomes, taken together, mean that professionals cannot be expected to carry on as they are. The time has come to fundamentally rethink our approach.

The opportunity to do things differently

> I need you to confront head-on the structures that are getting in the way of innovation and better outcomes ... It is a call to frontline staff and experts in the field to develop better ways of constructing and managing services ... I want to support and liberate you to improve faster, get better value for money, do the job you came into the profession to do. (Edward Timpson MP, Parliamentary Under-Secretary for Children and Families)[4]

Despite Munro's recommended transformation from a system 'over-bureaucratised and concerned with compliance to one that

---

[3] See: www.gov.uk/government/publications/progress-report-moving-towards-a-child-centred-system

[4] Parliamentary Under-Secretary Edward Timpson MP unveiling the children's services innovation programme, speaking to the Catch22 National Care Advisory Service (NCAS) conference about how innovative approaches can transform the life chances of vulnerable children and young people: 18 October 2013, Harrogate.

keeps a focus on children' (Munro, 2011, p 5), children and families services continue to be bureaucratic, compartmentalised and slow to respond to the needs of young people, families and the public. One year on from her initial review, Munro (2012) identified that while there were developments in the right direction, the pace of change needed to quicken. Munro observed that, as the result of changes to the NHS and reductions in spending, many areas were redesigning their services to improve families' 'access to the right help in a timely manner' (Munro, 2012, p 8). However, they were 'hampered by the continued presence of the statutory guidance and by the inspection process' (Munro, 2012, p 8).

Community Care (Cooper, 2013), two years after Munro's report, found that there was less optimism about the care system's potential to reform, asserting that 'little has changed for many social workers'. The Local Government Association (2013), in its *Rewiring public services* series, has argued that the 'current position [for children's services] is unsustainable: increasing demands on safeguarding and services for looked after children, combined with shifts in policy and funding, have resulted in councils' statutory duties and local accountability being woefully out of step with available resources and levers to influence' (p 5). Finally, the Association of Directors for Children's Services (2013), in a recent policy position paper exploring alternative models of care for adolescents, concluded that 'the current system provides neither value for money across the care sector – the outcomes do not justify the costs – nor a sufficiently clear expectation of what success should look like ... we continue to use care simply to "hold" some young people, and for short periods which are never likely to bring about lasting change' (p 6).

So, while the Working Together pilots have identified some early improvements, what is less apparent is the wholesale change in children's service delivery that places relationships at the centre envisaged by Munro. Ofsted asserts that good local authorities should have social workers who engage with families in a genuine relationship with clear purpose and boundaries. In its latest Social Care Annual Report (2012/13), many local authorities were found not to be meeting this standard: 'As it stands today, there are 20 councils where the standard of child protection is unacceptably poor and judged to be inadequate. In addition, there are 86 where these services are judged to be less than good' (Ofsted, 2013).

Catch22 has long held the view that success is determined largely by the way things are done and by creating the right kind of environment to deliver services. This can simply be expressed as a professional's time being well spent when it is focused on building trusting and strong connections with service users and their families or carers. The effectiveness of an intervention is based on the professional's ability to use the relationship to support the service user to identify for themselves the value of positive change and, in those teachable moments where the service user wants to make changes, help them navigate how to desist from engaging in negative behaviours and begin to engage in positive ones.

This behavioural change approach is based on evidence indicating that 'several factors common across treatments account for the bulk of the variance' in behaviour change (Mitchell, 2011). These common factors include: (a) beliefs, optimism, support networks and external strengths, and (b) the quality of the key worker. These have been proved to account for 40% and 30%, respectively, of fluctuation in changes in behaviour. These percentages are greater for those who are vulnerable and/or for clients for whom the relationship is the first stable one. Products such as assessment plans and programmes that emerge from the work a service user and key worker do together will only be as effective as the relationship itself. In practice, this could happen through key workers who co-ordinate with multiple agencies, meaning that families work intensively with one individual rather than with a multitude of agencies.

CommunityLinks (Bell, 2012), exploring the role of relationships in the delivery of public services, describes the value created when relationships in public services are effective in terms of improved service outcomes and wider benefits for service users as 'deep value'. Increasing the effectiveness of relationships becomes key to levering quality and performance. Based on the findings of its research, CommunityLinks asserts that 'effective relationships are not an added extra but are core to the delivery of effective services' (Bell, 2012, p 19). However, in terms of commissioning, this value is yet to become the norm in practice. Instead, Ofsted (2013) depicts a system under enormous pressure and intense scrutiny. From a provider perspective, this has resulted in a more risk-averse and consequently prescriptive approach to operating and commissioning services..

Probation, education and health have all faced similar criticisms of being bureaucratic, unresponsive and captured by the provider. In response, the government has sought to introduce levers and measures such as competition, choice, service user control and accountability. The aim is to give 'the professionals providing the service the freedom to respond imaginatively and innovatively to the competition that results' (HM Government, 2013, p i). For probation, the reforms set out in *Transforming rehabilitation* will see the creation of a National Probation Service for England and Wales whose responsibilities will include court assessments, enforcement and managing an estimated 20% of offenders deemed to be at high risk of harm – around 50,000 people. The remaining low- to medium-risk offenders – 80% of the cohort – will be managed by community rehabilitation companies (CRCs), drawn from the voluntary, community and social enterprise (VCSE) sector, private sector and mutuals, all of which will be allowed to bid for rehabilitation contracts (Ministry of Justice, 2013). The reforms aim to offer more scope for providers to innovate, with payment by results (PbR) acting as an incentive to focus on factors that support desistance and aim to rehabilitate the service user, such as employment, accommodation and substance misuse. Providers will have to prove their effectiveness in order to be paid and those unable to deliver improved outcomes will not win future contracts.

Children's services are not untouched by the forces of competition. Residential care and fostering, in particular, have been opened up to providers from the private and VCSE sectors, as well as mutuals. However, in this market, providers predominantly deliver to specifications (over)stated by the commissioners, who typically view the world through a public sector prism. This is reflected in service design. The consequence is that much of what social businesses like Catch22 deliver is constrained by the way services are designed.

Similarly, given the relative immaturity of this market, there is a lack of expertise among commissioners in relation to contract management. This creates an environment in which there is too great a focus on monitoring inputs and where providers can be over-managed rather than enabled to innovate on behalf of their service users. The current commissioning process is resource-intensive, both in terms of cost and staff time necessary, in preparing specifications and tenders that tick all of the procurement boxes rather than developing meaningful service delivery. Commissioners are too preoccupied with designing processes rather than enabling the outcomes they wish to see achieved.

In terms of commissioning, children's services are rarely system-wide services delivered by the VCSE sector. For example, only 3.6% of the costs of caring for looked-after children is attributed to VCSE organisations (Ross, 2012). The typical work of the VCSE sector is through small, short-term contracts, focused on specific problems and run as add-ons to public services provided by the state. Managing vulnerable groups such as children in need is typically viewed as the sole responsibility and expertise of the state. As debates around the future of the probation sector, the NHS and education have highlighted, VCSE organisations are often deemed unprepared and unable to deliver public services on a greater scale.

Commissioning and procurement arrangements have yet to fully explore the potential of PbR and greater accountability. PbR has been demonstrated to deliver improved outcomes in other arenas, including troubled families, criminal justice and health. A PbR framework, if properly applied to outcomes and quality, empowers the professional. There will be those who argue that it is potentially unethical to make profit from children's services. However, in response, it could be argued that to continue to deliver more of the same and expect different outcomes is also wrong and there is a significant cost connected to failure. Where VCSE organisations are able to drive up outcomes, the reward will be their ability to reinvest in their services, ultimately boosting the skills, knowledge and ability of the workforce through training, learning and continued investment.

Putting professionals in the driving seat

As demand for services increases, with a growing population and an economic environment where financial resources are under serious pressure, it could be argued that this is a once-in-a-generation opportunity to do things differently, with a view to empowering professionals, improving outcomes, producing more responsive services designed around needs and achieving more with limited resources.

So, what are the key elements of a service delivery model that can realise Munro's vision of a 'work environment that will better support professionals in giving children and young people the help they need' (Munro, 2012, p 3)?

Placing the power of the relationship for effecting change at the centre of all models of support

Building strong, one-to-one relationships has to be a central plank in any model of support. As touched on earlier, the strength of the relationship between service user and their caseworker is pivotal to the effectiveness of the intervention. In practice, this can be enabling for key workers who co-ordinate with multiple agencies, meaning that one individual, rather than a multitude of agencies, works intensively with families and can be a constant contact in otherwise chaotic lives.

Co-design and co-production

To realise services in which professionals are truly bought closer to the service user, providers need to have a greater role in shaping specifications, designing solutions and co-producing with public sector partners. This approach recognises that while the state plays a vital role in protecting children and young people from harm, it need not do everything itself to achieve this goal and should consider which non-state providers can provide better quality services. We believe that a more effective commissioning system is one in which the state is left to define its statutory responsibilities, acts as an enabler and facilitator for others to provide services, and judges providers on whether they have met specified outcomes. The state would leave the provider, based on their professional expertise and experience, to innovate, design more flexible and responsive services, and work in collaboration with other agencies to draw together the relevant talents.

However, to realise this vision, the VCSE sector needs to be treated as a genuine partner in the delivery of public services (not just in small parts of a service) and assessed on its track record of managing risk (in terms of risk to the public and financial risks), its ability to understand and work within legislation, and its expertise in working with vulnerable and challenging groups.

Organisations like Catch22 can act to leverage support from foundations, charitable trusts, and the corporate and business world, as well as maximise the capacity of communities themselves to contribute to service delivery through assets such as the knowledge of local partners and communities, volunteers, and social networks. This intimate and long-standing connection with communities and service users can help drive greater responsiveness through service user experience and feedback in the co-production and co-design of services, which are a natural extension of the positive role of the relationship.

Focus on early intervention and prevention

The service delivery model must improve responses to children who have been identified as having a need. The current system is not good enough at triggering consistent responses when it comes into contact with children in need; instead, it has been designed to focus on those perceived to be at greatest risk. Given the statutory requirements associated with this group, the resources follow children in state care. While understandable, this results in the emergency group getting increasingly larger as the system acts to feed itself, and children in need without adequate support become children in care. This begs the question of how we differentiate our responses to the two groups. We believe, as a starting point, there is the potential to draw on approaches outlined in *Transforming rehabilitation*, where those at highest risk are managed by the state and those at low to medium risk are managed by mutual, private and VCS providers offering a positive solution.

Attracting the right kind of people

The new framework would allow professionals to do their job well, to be excited to go to work every day, to be free to concentrate on the person and not feel scared that they are not fulfilling the required processes. The kinds of people we want to work with in this new world are those who are passionate about social justice. The new framework should encourage behaviours that are risk-aware, entrepreneurial and fleet of foot, focused on outcomes and rooted in the evidence base.

Post-Munro, we need staff who are empathetic and entrepreneurial, curious and brave, proactive, self-aware and, most importantly, focused on the needs of the children they work with.

Case studies

Wirral

At the intensive family support service in the Wirral, Catch22 helps families in need of extra support, including families affected by substance dependency, domestic violence or who have been involved in antisocial behaviour. The family is allocated a dedicated Catch22 support worker who starts by assessing what they need help with. Based on this assessment, a plan is made to which the whole family agrees. The Catch22 worker then co-ordinates with other agencies to ensure the family receives support for everything they need help with. The plan is reviewed every six weeks, by Catch22, the family and the other agencies involved. We support the families for six to 12 months and follow up with each family six months after closure.

Catch22's core offer to families includes:

- assigning a key worker to the family;
- identifying the needs of the family;
- working with a full range of needs, both practical and emotional;
- agreeing a clear plan with the family and ensuring that all members stick to it;

- identifying and working with partners, drawing in a range of expertise and referring families to other agencies where necessary;
- a flexible approach, including early morning and late night visits, responding to the needs of the family but ensuring that challenges are made.

Families have seen a 91% reduction in the number of incidents of domestic violence, an 83% reduction in antisocial behaviour and offending, a 67% reduction in alcohol, drug and volatile substance abuse by children, and an 83% improvement in children and young people's attendance and behaviour at school (Catch22, 2012).

Northamptonshire Rapid Response Service

Working in partnership with Northamptonshire County Council, Catch22 has developed a service designed to support families in times of acute stress. The service works intensively with 10 families at any one time. Support is normally provided in the family's home and will be offered outside normal office hours, arranged to match the current needs of the family and further needs as they arise. Support is limited to a maximum of 14 days for each family, although this can be extended in exceptional circumstances. Support is intensive, with staff sometimes spending five hours a day with the family during the period of intervention. Workers make contact with the family on the day of referral within five hours of its receipt. The team identifies individual pressure points in families and works with them to develop successful coping strategies. In the first year of operation, the team has worked with 160 children, of whom only eight had to be received into local authority care.

Such models lend themselves to social investment vehicles that, if delivered at scale, could lead to a significant reconfiguring in the way children's services budgets are utilised.

Conclusion

In an environment in which expectations about supporting vulnerable and challenging children and young people are higher than ever, where demand is increasing but resources are finite, we cannot continue to tinker around the edges of a system that is not empowering our most important asset – our staff – nor maximising what the evidence suggests works. The time has come for bold decisions to be made and new paths forged. It will be challenging for many but doing the same thing year on year is likely to deliver the same results.

I understand why there is a reluctance to open up the market to new ways of delivering services and to trust the everyday running and delivery of services to others. However, we must focus on the reasons why we should embrace doing this – for the service users who deserve to realise their ambitions, for the professionals who are allowed to flourish in their roles and ultimately for the taxpayer who deserves better value for money.

There will be challenges. The new system needs to ensure that the formal mechanisms for working together to safeguard and promote the welfare of children, and the lines of accountability within and between different organisations, are as clear and unambiguous as possible. Despite these challenges, we see the provision of public services differently, where the golden thread is closer links between the service user and the service provider.

References

Association of Directors for Children's Services (ADCS) (2013) 'What is care for? Alternative models of care for adolescents', position statement. Available at: www.adcs.org.uk/download/position-statements/2013/ADCS_position_statement_What_Is_Care_For_April_2013.pdf

Bell, K. (2012) 'Deep value – the role of effective relationships in public services', CommunityLinks. Available at: www.community-links.org/linksuk/?p=2367#sthash.IRXv2IaL.dpuf

Catch22 (2012) *Catch22 impact report, 2011/2012*, London: Catch22.

Children's Commissioner (2012) *Inquiry into child sexual exploitation in gangs and groups* [online], London: Children's Commissioner. Available at: www.childrenscommissioner.gov.uk/info/csegg1

Cooper, J. (2013) 'The Munro report two years on: social workers find little has changed', *Community Care*], 19 February. Available at: www.communitycare.co.uk/2013/02/19/the-munro-report-two-years-on-social-workers-find-little-has-changed/

Department for Communities and Local Government (2013) *The fiscal case for working with troubled families*, London: DCLG.

Department of Health (2012) 'Preventing suicide in England: a cross-government outcomes strategy to save lives'. Available at: www.gov.uk/government/publications/suicide-prevention-strategy-forengland

Glenndenning, J. (2013) *Children looked after in England (including adoption and care leavers), year ending 31 March 2013*, London: DfE.

HM Government (2011) *Open public services*, White Paper, Cm 8145, London: HMSO.

HM Government (2013) *Open public services, 2013*, London: HMSO.

Knox, G. (2012) *Characteristics of children in need in England, 2011–12*, London: DfE.

Local Government Association (2013) *Rewiring public services: children's services*, London: LGA.

Ministry of Justice (2013) *Transforming rehabilitation: principles of competition*, London: MoJ.

Mitchell, P.F. (2011) 'Evidence-based practice in real-world services for young people with complex needs: new opportunities suggested by recent implementation science', *Children and Youth Services Review*, 33, 207–16.

Munro, E. (2011) *The Munro review of child protection. Final report: a child-centred system*, London: DfE.

Munro, E. (2012) *The Munro review of child protection. Progress report: moving towards a child centred system*, London: DfE.

Ofsted (Office for Standards in Education) (2013) Speech by Sir Michael Wilshaw HMCI launching *The Social Care Annual Report*, 15 October, Church House, Westminster.

Prison Reform Trust (2013) *Prison: the facts; Bromley briefings, summer 2013*, Bromley, London: PRT.

Ross, N. (2012) *Local authority and school expenditure on education; children's services and social care for 2010–11, including school revenue balances*, London: DfE.

Timpson, E. (2013) 'How innovative approaches can transform the life chances of vulnerable children and young people,' NCAS conference, 18 October, Harrogate.

4

Re-imagining early help: looking forward, looking back

Sue White, Kate Morris, Brid Featherstone, Marian Brandon and June Thoburn

It is irresponsible not to look back and ask — how did we get here, what has been learned and what has been lost? (Stevenson, 2013, p 98)

Social workers in England remain a vital support for many children and families. They also serve to protect children at risk, making many wise and humane decisions. However, all is not well. Some decisions are not so wise and not so humane and many of these are a product of poorly designed organisational systems and inappropriate institutional cultures. Statutory social work is caught in a perpetual tension between the rights of the many to help and to freedom from unwelcome scrutiny and intrusive intervention in the intimate spaces of family life and the rights of the relatively few who come to serious harm. The precautionary principle is in a constantly discursive and moral dance with proportionality. Each violent and, when viewed retrospectively, tragically preventable death has its own effect on this fickle pendulum. For at least two decades it has swung in a particular direction. Efforts to embed early help more widely in the children's workforce may have been apparent under New Labour in the various *Every child matters* documentation (Department for Education and Skills, 2003). However, the terms 'social work' and 'social worker' were conspicuously absent from this swathe of material, which emphasised the non-stigmatising nature of support for children's 'additional needs', which were to fall below the threshold of statutory social work. In recent years, social work has become increasingly distanced from most forms of early help and become more strongly identified with child protection, with increased anxiety that support for families will be perceived as losing sight of the child.

For social work, the policy response to high-profile events has been to standardise processes and seek 'consistent thresholds'. This, it has been argued, would ensure safety in the system. In fact, it has led to a great deal of 'screening' behaviour and short-term, multiple assessments in children's services, often at the expense of practical help and sustained relational support (Featherstone et al, 2013). In reality, consistent thresholds are unachievable and, in a dynamic system, probably an entirely undesirable preoccupation. Thresholds are responsive to system demands and available resources and are affected by a range of human, social and organisational factors (Munro, 2011; Platt and Turney, 2013). For example, detailed analysis of the system has demonstrated that, as referral rates increase, the number of 'non-urgent' cases allocated falls (Broadhurst et al, 2009). The actors in the system perfectly rationally prioritise risk. In such a system, an immobile baby presenting at the emergency department with a fractured skull and no explanation will always make it over the threshold whatever the competing demand, but most children and families referred to social work services are not in such a category. A family struggling to cope is also going to struggle to get through the front door of many local authority children's social care services and they are going to struggle harder on some days than on others. Yet, a great deal of organisational time is spent crafting 'thresholds', creating colourful typologies of various 'tiers' of need and eligibility; as a consequence, waste enters the system as universal services try to second-guess responses (Masson and Dickens, 2013).

This preoccupation with compliance and efficiency has coalesced with a decoupling of the child from their family in a child-focused orientation (Gilbert et al, 2011). This orientation concentrates on the child as an individual in independent relation to the state. In such an orientation, children's relationships with siblings, their parents, their family networks, friends and neighbourhoods become background. The complexities of relational identities, past, present and future, are glossed; indeed, as we are seeing in England currently, a powerful moral mandate can be provided for a child rescue project, reinforced by every terrible death. It is important to remember that these developments differ from the philosophy and organisation of services historically established in England. The reorganisation of personal social services in 1971 was based on the recommendations of the Seebohm report:

> The new local authority departments would be a community-based and family-oriented service which would be available to all. The new department will, we believe, reach far beyond the discovery and rescue of social casualties; it will enable the greatest possible number of individuals to act reciprocally, giving and receiving service for the wellbeing of the whole community. (Seebohm, 1968, para 2)

The new departments would be universal in nature, focusing on the family and community, and they would provide a range of personalised, generic services. Importantly, the family was the unit on which the service would be based (Hall et al, 2010). In England, not anymore.

Though focusing specifically on families with children, the Children Act 1989 sought to maintain a balance between working collaboratively to support families at times of stress and intervening coercively to protect children only when necessary (Tunstill et al, 2010). But, Tunstill et al note, 20 years later, the mandate to seek to work in partnership with parents is low on the list of priorities. Let us take a look at what happens in practice in our system in England, with its child-centric orientation and its effect on early and ongoing help.

Case study

Mary is a team manager in a referral and assessment team. She receives a contact from the police about a domestic incident the previous night. This morning, so far, she has 20 other contacts in her inbox. There have been four previous contacts about this family and two assessments over the past two years. On both occasions the case was immediately closed. Mary decides to ask Jo to visit. Jo has been qualified for two years. The office from which the team works is in the centre of town, based above the 'one-stop shop' access point for local authority services. The council's policy of hot-desking means there is little clutter on desks. It is perfect white space, corporately pristine. There are few personalised areas and Jo may be sitting with different people each day. Jo visits the estate where the family live in her car. She has never walked around the estate, shopped there or stopped for a coffee, sandwich or a drink. Indeed, there are few places to buy food and drink. There is a children's centre, which she has visited for meetings, but she has no time to be involved in any of the activities run there. When she visits the family, she is very aware of the importance of seeing and talking to the children, but this is difficult when she is responding to an incident of domestic abuse, where people are upset, and the children are both under three years old. Jo works very hard to adopt a firm and consistent approach with parents. She is always aware of the dangers of being too trusting of their accounts or becoming too involved with them, though their problems are often obvious and pressing. She is careful to keep the conversation this morning very clearly focused on the children's welfare. She explains the impact of domestic abuse on children, asks about the circumstances of the previous night's events and runs through sections of the initial assessment record. She returns to her office to record all her activities diligently and reinforces her accountability for her actions in supervision. The children were in bed, the incident involved shouting, nobody was physically hurt. The relationship is very volatile but stable. There is no history of violence. The case is closed.

Based on our research, this is a typical response to 'low-level' concerns and the system in which Mary and Jo work demands it to be so. Workflow is king. It is the only way to keep the show on the road. This is the everyday world of social work practice with children and families in England. Its moral mandate is clear enough, but what are the effects of this system design and the underpinning ethos on children, families and social workers themselves? While boxes are ticked and the 'right' people are seen and talked to, we suggest that too high a price is being paid by children, families and social workers. Although the system is ostensibly all about them, children and young people seldom self-refer, and they tell researchers that when they are troubled, they prefer to seek help from those they know and trust (or helplines where they can remain anonymous). They tell of their fear of talking to social workers as they may lose control over what is done and how.

Our research with parents and wider family networks suggests that encounters are experienced as frightening and deficit-focused (Morris, 2011). Moreover, their distrust of services can be furthered when they see social workers operating within an instrumental approach that treats them as means rather than ends: they are considered only insofar as their actions/inactions impact on children, not as people in their own right. They know and resent it when no attempt is made to understand them as relational, emoting beings, and there is apparently little appreciation of their everyday struggles in a context of little money and neighbourhoods with rapidly disappearing facilities.

It is particularly urgent in the current climate of austerity that we engage with the centrality of everyday struggle in the lives of families. Some of the key issues that emerged from Hooper et al's (2007) study on the links between poverty and maltreatment are important to restate and to reflect on in the contemporary context where poverty is increasing (Ridge, 2013). Compared to other research on parents in poverty, there were high levels of stress in the sample, reflecting the impact of poverty and associated issues such as poor or overcrowded housing and the frequency of other forms of adversity, including childhood maltreatment, domestic violence, relationship breakdown, bereavement and mental health issues. The life story approach used allowed for the exploration of the accumulation of disadvantage over a life: 'Some life experiences made poverty more difficult to manage and poverty made all other forms of adversity more difficult to cope with' (Hooper et al, 2007, p 32). Parenting was an important source of identity, self-worth and satisfaction for most, and an absence of other socially valued roles or sense of identity and self-worth could make it difficult to seek or accept help with parenting difficulties, particularly when the system is explicitly child-focused. However, both unresolved abuse and ongoing abuse left some parents struggling to exercise control and authority over their lives in terms of partnerships, parenting and managing on a low income. Some women who became parents as a result of rape had a particularly difficult relationship with their children. Children with behaviour problems posed particular problems, especially in overcrowded conditions. Mothers with histories of childhood abuse and/or domestic violence felt further victimised by children who were aggressive and violent towards them and other children and found such children extremely difficult to manage.

Hooper et al (2007) found that parents' own experiences of violence and abuse had ongoing impacts on their lives and were interwoven with poverty in a range of ways. Defensive investments in identity as a parent, reflecting a lack of alternatives as a result of poverty, are of interest and link with the concerns raised by Featherstone (1999) about the restricted notions of subjectivity afforded women and mothers. It is difficult to make space for women to admit they regret being a mother and/or do not enjoy it. For some women, restricted opportunities in education and occupational advancement mean motherhood is not necessarily 'freely' chosen, and this is compounded by rearing living, breathing children with obvious needs in difficult economic circumstances. For such women, other mothers, friends and family members may not be sources of support but indeed sources of condemnation or, if feelings are left unvoiced, sources of guilt or fear.

The 'spoiled' identities associated with poverty and other life experiences can lead to social isolation. The need for recognition and respect, often denied to people living in poverty and those who experience forms of adversity such as violence and abuse, could make children's behavioural problems and sometimes just ordinary lack of respect difficult to bear or manage. Children's actions such as running away or wanting contact with an ex-partner could impede the capacity to protect, especially when social, financial and personal resources are stretched. Finally, services could compound feelings of powerlessness, especially when practical resources (such as housing) are not dealt with.

Hooper et al (2007) found in discussion with professionals that poverty often slipped out of sight as they focused on drug or alcohol problems and on individual attitudes, values and priorities:

> A limited conception of poverty, lack of resources to address it, and lack of attention to the impacts of trauma, addiction and lifelong disadvantage on the choices that people experience themselves as having may contribute to overemphasising agency at the expense of structural inequality.' (Hooper et al, 2007, p 97)

So, where do the complex conversations about everyday coping, insecure relationships, maternal ambivalence, jealousy, anxiety or fear of abandonment take place in current models of service delivery? There is little space in the social worker's diary. Typically, families are 'signposted' to other services, but how are these designed and configured and their efforts rewarded by renewed contracts?

Prevention and early help

Preventive and early help services have also been affected by political position-taking and the moralisation of parenting. The emergence of national, large-scale preventive programmes came, in part, as a response to analysis of the consequences of social exclusion. These were set within the rise of what was described as 'the social investment state' (Fawcett et al, 2004), with the end goal of economically and socially active citizens. Various theories of social exclusion supported the analysis of pathways that led to what was deemed to be a constellation of poor outcomes, including worklessness, poor health, crime and low educational attainment. While the concept of social exclusion is contested, with Levitas (2005) suggesting that different forms and understandings of exclusion can be identified and the argument for its usefulness in prevention critiqued (Axford, 2010), the central role the concept played in the wave of prevention programmes initiated by New Labour cannot be underestimated.

With this new paradigm, as in local authority children's services, the positioning of the child as a recipient of investment for the future shaped policy discourse. The development of preventive programmes such as Sure Start resulted from this political interest in notions of predictive risk (Morris, 2011). The Sure Start programme was imported from the US and replicated Head Start, a programme rooted in an analysis of the impact of poverty and low-income environments on children's capacities to reach their potential and long-term outcomes. The UK Sure Start model adopted the US approach of targeting, using local and national administrative data to identify geographical areas of deprivation. The original roll-out of Sure Start in England held tight to the intention of delineating specific localities for the programme and thereby provided the opportunity for comparative and experimental design impact research. The Children's Fund followed hard on the heels of the implementation of Sure Start and while also badged as a response to the outcomes of social exclusion, had different antecedents and political influences. The programme in part emerged from political exasperation with the failure of local authorities to implement fully Part III (the family support provisions) of the Children Act 1989 (Policy Action Team Report 12). This, coupled with awareness that children aged 5–11 years were under-represented in other allied developments, led to the development of the programme. Driven initially by the Treasury, the programme sought to tackle the 'consequences of social exclusion and build pathways out of poverty' (CYPU, 2002). Unusually, the programme did not stipulate a menu of interventions or models; instead, local partnerships were formed and were required to devise local services that reflected their mapping of local need. They were, however, expected to generate an evidence base using local evaluation arrangements. It was intended that by adopting the framework, those seeking to develop prevention programmes could examine and, if necessary, challenge the underlying values and assumptions informing their provision.

The possibilities of innovative and 'inductive' evaluations were, however, subsequently derailed by the rise of 'prevention science' and evidence-based early intervention programmes. The evidence from the National Evaluation of the Children's Fund (NECF) and the National Evaluation of Sure Start (NESS) that families with complex and acute needs failed to engage with the prevention programmes (debates can be had about whether the services failed the families; see Morris, 2011) or that the restricted capacity of the families meant engagement was difficult (Edwards et al, 2006) led to a refocusing of political attention. Two themes emerged in this new policy landscape: the desire to target services more effectively and the need to ensure that programmes adopted had a robust 'evidence base'. The 'what works?' question became increasingly prominent when decisions about funding were made, and the 'commissioner' (often without a background in social work or social care) became increasingly powerful.

In the UK, the rise and rise of evidence-based prevention programmes is readily apparent in the influential Allen reports (Allen, 20011a, 2011b). These reports, commissioned by the government, set out a series of recommendations for the adoption of 'tested' early interventions to support children to fulfil their social and emotional potential. It is thus argued that children are equipped to become better parents in later years and that transmitted 'cycles of dysfunction' can be broken (Allen, 2011a). Early intervention is employed as a state mechanism for ensuring that later costs to the economy and to the state are avoided. The Allen assessment of the efficacy of this approach is augmented by his analysis that sets out the purported consequences for children's brains and the subsequent psychosocial development of a failure to intervene early to transform inadequate parenting and family life (Wastell and White, 2012). The moral message of the Allen report is clear:

> Parents who are neglectful, or who are drunk, drugged or violent, will have impaired capacity to provide this social and emotional stability, and will create the likelihood that adverse experiences might have a negative impact on their children's development ... the worst and deepest damage is done to children when their brains are being formed during their earliest months and years. (Allen, 2011a, p 15)

This refocusing of prevention towards early intervention and a narrow version of evidence-based practice is likely to dilute further the attention that policymakers and researchers pay to adverse social and economic pressures, and hence to everyday coping. The rise in experimental design research programmes had a symbiotic relationship with the rise of 'prevention science' and facilitated the emergence of methodological debates about programme fidelity and researcher bias.

This methodological preoccupation reached its high-water mark in the aforementioned Allen reports. The reports represent the pinnacle of the cost-effectiveness commissioning paradigm. No doubt understanding the potent rhetorical force, Allen's arguments are predicated on economics. Services must yield to interrogation by the randomised control trial (RCT) and only the RCT will count as evidence.

Allen is aware that this formula may jeopardise many UK home-grown services and interventions, privileging those from the US in particular. His answer to this problem, however, is to prescribe for UK services better 'experimental' methods. The interventions must be made to fit the method, not the other way round:

> Like many UK early intervention programmes, Nottingham Life Skills has been evaluated many times, always with promising results, but it will need to use a method, such as randomised controlled trial, to meet the standards of evidence used in my review, devised by internationally renowned practitioners such as Delbert Elliott and Steve Aos.... This evaluation would produce the specific estimate of impact on children's social and emotional health that is fundamental to the kind of economic analysis required for public and private sectors to feel confident about investing. What the Nottingham Life Skills programme currently lacks, in common with many other excellent UK-designed Early Intervention programmes, is an 'effect size', which the economists can plug into their models used in advising investors about where to get the best return of their scarce resources. (Allen, 2011a, p 77)

So, Nottingham Life Skills works; except it does not. Blewett and Tunstill (2013) dub this preoccupation 'outcomes theology'. Allen seems unaware of the changes that would need to be made to the Nottingham Life Skills project to make it amenable to an RCT and the resources necessary to make this happen. He is keen to invoke the US experts but, in so doing, he manages to gloss over the nuances of their own positions. The following is taken from an online interview in 2011 with Delbert Elliott, Director of the Center for the Study and Prevention of Violence at the University of Colorado, which is noteworthy for its nuanced humaneness and critical perspective on the timescales imposed by the very commissioning paradigm that is in charge over here:

> Unfortunately, the whole mechanism for funding these programs is not good. The grant goes for three years and then the program goes away. That's why we're in Montbello, to try to get the agencies to continue the funding after the grant ends. The opposite side is that no program works 100% of the time. The discouraging part is that there are kids who go into the programs and come out the other side and nothing has really changed. The issues tend to be environmental conditions they have to live with that could be changed. The heartbreaking part is that it doesn't have to be that way. If we could commit the necessary resources, we could change their lives. (See http://connections.cu.edu/news/five-questions-for-delbert-elliott/)

The trouble is that one cannot design an RCT for those kinds of community-based interventions, or for simple forms of 'ordinary help'. In fact, the more ordinary and relatively cheap the help, the less likely it is to yield to experimental methods. In particular, the imperative for 'programme fidelity' jeopardises the supple adaptability needed to help families facing multiple problems. This is underscored in a recent evaluation of the Westminster family recovery project (Thoburn et al, 2013):

> Our conclusions do not support one of the key premises that underpinned the original *Think family* tender documents (still in evidence in some recent English government initiatives; see Allen, 2011a) that experimentally evaluated 'model programmes' requiring programme fidelity should be central to service provision. At least with respect to work with very troubled families who are either 'hard to engage' or 'hard to change', we conclude that the lack of flexibility in this approach risks impeding family engagement. (p 235)

Furthermore, Thoburn et al (2013) note the importance of ordinary practical help with finances and housing. In so doing, they underscore our earlier points. What counts as valid knowledge has a direct effect on what counts as a valid service. So, what are we to do as a profession about the distorting effects of the politics of research and how can we best ensure that struggling families receive appropriate relationship-based help for an appropriate period of time?

Doing things differently

We have noted that, in recent decades, we have moved decisively away from neighbourhood-based teams that typically incorporated community development approaches. Jack and Gill (2010) offer practical examples of such approaches from previous decades. Neighbourhood-based social workers adopted a community development approach to reduce the pressures on parents and their children by enhancing the range of activities and informal social supports available to them. Jack and Gill note that a five-year evaluation of one project found there had been significant reductions in the numbers of children in care or on supervision orders and that numbers on the child protection register had fallen to almost zero. The workers had helped not only to increase the levels of informal activities and social supports, but also to reduce mistrust between parents and workers so that help was sought earlier.

In a climate of austerity, with deep cuts to local authority budgets and the widespread dismantling of long-standing community-based services like youth work, the national Troubled Families payment-by-results initiative is offering unexpected opportunities for a new type of early help for families. The initiative also offers the possibility for social work to re-establish a firmer footing in preventive and supportive work that nudges the thresholds of statutory services for children's social care. The key outcomes of improved school attendance, reduction in criminality and getting adults into work demanded by the scheme are more than challenging but early successes and satisfaction from families are being reported in some local and national evaluations (Jones et al, 2013; Thoburn et al, 2013). Family change is being attributed (including by Louise Casey, Head of the Troubled Families scheme, in a recent *Guardian* interview) to the good relationships that develop between families and workers.

Building relationships is, and has always been, at the heart of good social work practice. Social work needs to reclaim these roots and demonstrate that the profession has something to offer to support this type of early help service and to re-establish its own identity. As Olive Stevenson notes in the quotation at the beginning of this chapter, it is irresponsible not to look backwards before we look forward. We have much to rediscover, including conversation. Using the learning from the Westminster family recovery project (Thoburn et al, 2013), the wider London tri-borough set up part of its Troubled Families scheme as a family coaching service, where families with complex needs are visited and helped by a skilled and experienced, but not typically social work-qualified, 'coach' one or more times a week for approximately six months. Early findings from an evaluation of this service show that relationship-based work with the whole family is satisfying for family and coach alike and is meeting the Troubled Families outcomes (Brandon and Sorensen, 2013). However, there are risks and faultlines appearing. As well as finding the work satisfying, it is also difficult, emotionally draining and stressful for the coaches, who can quickly become demoralised and lose confidence when family change is not sustained (Brandon and Sorensen, 2013). Managing the complex feelings associated with work with families in difficulties is familiar territory for social workers, who can have formal roles alongside or as part of services like this, offering emotional support, supervision, consultation and sometimes co-working. Social work oversight can also help family coaches or outreach workers recognise when a different level of expertise is needed and the case needs to be 'stepped up', such as in 'edge of care' cases. In this way, children in need of protection can be picked up quickly. Social work is steeped in managing risk and uncertainty and early help services need this expertise from social work as much as social work needs to connect back with its relationship roots, whether this is within statutory services or the third sector.

When we make these arguments, we are often accused of invoking a 'golden age'. Maybe this is the case but, whatever their metal, the systems that currently dominate practice are terribly tarnished by the relentless pursuit of efficiency through standardised processes and risk-averse individualist practices. Corporate front doors are often slammed shut, rupturing relationships at all levels. Violence has been done to relational social work. Of course, history does not repeat itself but sometimes it rhymes. It is time to retune!

Acknowledgements

Some of the ideas in this chapter formed part of a blog by Brid Featherstone, Sue White and Kate Morris, 'Moving from the individual to the relational', in 2013. Available at http://relationalwelfare.com/2013/10/28/moving-from-the-individual-to-the-relational-child-protection-re-imagined/

References

Allen, G. (2011a) *Early intervention: the next steps. An independent report to Her Majesty's Government*, London: HMSO.

Allen, G. (2011b) *Early intervention: smart investments, massive savings. An independent report to Her Majesty's Government*, London: HMSO.

Axford, N. (2010) 'Is social exclusion a useful concept in children's services?', *British Journal of Social Work*, 40(3), 737–54.

Blewett, J. and Tunstill, J. (2013) 'Mapping the journey: outcome-focused practice and the role of interim outcomes in family support services', *Child and Family Social Work Online Early*, doi:10.1111/cfs.12073, p 1.

Brandon, M. and Sorensen, P. (2013) *Evaluation of the tri-borough family coaching service: interim report*, Norwich: University of East Anglia.

Broadhurst, K., Wastell, D., White, S., Hall, C., Peckover, S., Thompson, K., Pithouse, A. and Davey, D. (2010) 'Performing "initial assessment": identifying the latent conditions for error at the front-door of local authority children's services', *British Journal of Social Work*, 40(2), 352-70.

CYPU (Children and Young People's Unit) (2002) *The Children's Fund guidance*, London: DfES.

DfES (Department for Education and Skills) (2003) *Every child matters*, London: The Stationery Office.

Edwards, A., Barnes, M., Morris, K. and Plewis, I. (2006) *Working to prevent the social exclusion of children and young people: final lessons from the National Evaluation of the Children's Fund*, Research Report 734, London: DfES.

Fawcett, B., Featherstone, F. and Goddard, J. (2004) *Contemporary child care policy and practice*, Basingstoke: Palgrave Macmillan.

Featherstone, B. (1999) 'Taking mothering seriously: the implications for child protection', *Child and Family Social Work*, 4(1), 43–55.

Featherstone, B., Morris, K. and White, S. (2013) 'A marriage made in hell: child protection meets early intervention', *British Journal of Social Work*, doi:10.1093/bjsw/bct052, pp 1–15.

Gilbert, N., Parton, N. and Skiveness, M. (2011) 'Changing patterns of responses and emerging orientations', in N. Gilbert, N. Parton and M. Skiveness (eds) *Child protection systems: international trends and orientations*, Oxford: Oxford University Press.

Hall, C., Parton, N., Peckover, S. and White, S. (2010) 'Child-centric ICTs and the fragmentation of child welfare practice in England', *Journal of Social Policy*, 39(3), 393–413.

Hooper, C.-A., Gorin, S., Cabral, C. and Dyson, C. (2007) *Living with hardship 24/7: the diverse experiences of families in poverty in England*, London: The Frank Buttle Trust.

Jack, G. and Gill, O. (2010) 'The role of communities in safeguarding children and young people', *Child Abuse Review*, 19, 82–96.

Jones, R., Matczak, A., Davies, K. and Byford, I. (2013) *Wandsworth Family Recovery project: the views of families and other agencies*, London: Kingston University.

—

Masson, J. and Dickens, J. (2013) *Partnership by law? The pre-proceedings process for families on the edge of care proceedings*, Report of ESRC RES-062-2226, https://lred.uea.ac.uk/documents/3437903/0/full+report+preproceedings+process.pdf/4bf882b3-2f34-4c46-9f67-63bb37deff2d

Morris, K. (2011) 'Family support: policies for practice', in M. Davis (ed) *Social work with children and families*, Basingstoke: Palgrave MacMillan.

Munro, E. (2011) *The Munro review of child protection. Final report: a child-centred system*, London: DfE.

Platt, D. and Turney, D. (2013) 'Making threshold decisions in child protection: a conceptual analysis', *British Journal of Social Work*, doi: 10.1093/bjsw/bct007, first published online 14 February 2013.

Ridge, T. (2013) 'We are all in this together? The hidden costs of poverty, recession and austerity policies on Britain's poorest children', *Children and Society*, 27, 406–17.

Seebohm, F. (1968) *Report of the Committee on Local Authority and Allied Social Services*, Cm 3703, London: HMSO.

Stevenson, O. (2013) *Reflections on a life in social work: a personal and professional memoir*, Buckingham: Hinton House.

Thoburn, J., Cooper, N., Brandon, M. and Connolly, S. (2013) 'The place of "think family" approaches in child and family social work: messages from a process evaluation of an English "pathfinder" service', *Children and Youth Services Review*, 35(2), 228–36.

Tunstill, J., Thoburn, J. and Aldgate, J. (2010) 'Promoting and safeguarding the welfare of children: a bridge too far?', *Journal of Children's Services* 5(3), 14–24.

Wastell, D. and White, S. (2012) 'Blinded by neuroscience: social policy, the family and the infant brain', *Families, Relationships and Society*, 1(3), 397–414.

—

5

Children should be seen and heard: understanding the child's experience

Jenny Clifton

Eileen Munro's review of child protection stressed the importance of child-centred practice and framed an effective system in terms of children's right to safety (Munro, 2011, 2012). To observe the principles outlined in her final report, adult helpers need to understand and respond to each child as an individual, to work with them and to measure the effectiveness of help from the child's experience. This chapter looks at what child-centred practice might mean from a child's perspective, drawing on two recent research projects undertaken for the Office of the Children's Commissioner (OCC): children's views on 'telling' about abuse (Cossar et al, 2013) and a review of the impact of parental alcohol misuse (Adamson and Templeton, 2012). We did not set out to measure whether things have improved for children since the Munro review, but we believe that their perspectives will assist those asking and answering that question.

What does child-centred practice really mean?

Child-centred practice is rights-based practice. Under the United Nations Convention on the Rights of the Child (UNCRC), children have rights to protection, support and participation. These rights are interwoven and interdependent: effective protection takes account of children's own understanding of their needs, how they protect themselves, and their perception of what needs to change in their family. Conceiving protection and safety as children's basic rights can help professionals to stay focused on the child (Clifton, 2012).

Obstacles to such a focus have been identified as: helplessness or fear in the face of antagonistic parents; lack of confidence in challenging them or more influential colleagues; and lack of skills, time or knowledge of abuse or child development. The fears felt by professionals should provoke worries about the child who lives and manages such anxiety daily but they need skilled and supportive supervision to make sense of this and to learn how to develop working partnerships with parents while firmly putting the child's needs first.

Through getting to know each child well, and combining this with knowledge from research, developmental theory and professional experience, the practitioner can 'get inside' the child's experience. Gillian Schofield, discussing the relevance of attachment theory to work with children, points to the importance of 'mind-mindedness' (a term she attributes to Miens [1997]): 'Tuning into the thoughts and feelings of this particular child in this particular context' (Schofield, 2008, p 45).

Giving children a voice is valuable both in the overall fulfilment of their rights and in directly helping them. Finding a language for self-expression can in itself assist a child to process difficult experiences and help restore their self-esteem. This is where the engagement of the helper with the child is so important. Child-centred practice is relationship-based practice: when children are asked what matters to them, they often rate highly the need for trusting and lasting relationships with adults who care for them. This message comes across powerfully from the perspectives of the children and young people who contributed to the research presented here.

What might help children to tell about abuse and get help at an earlier stage?

It was discussions with young people who wished to contribute to the Munro review that led the OCC to consider the routes along which young people might find their way from risk and harm to safety, and to look at the obstacles in their way. Many children do not tell anyone about the abuse they suffer, at least not until adulthood, as recent high-profile investigations have confirmed. There is evidence that many children will disclose abuse but not all will be heard and they often delay for years before telling anyone (Allnock and Miller, 2013). Other studies have shown that older children and young people are not getting help because they are assumed to be more 'resilient' (Rees et al, 2010). Such concerns led the OCC to commission research on the experience of children and young people themselves in order to find out what might make it more likely that children would tell someone at an earlier stage and what response would make it more possible for them to get help. We called the project 'Recognition and Telling' and the research was commissioned from the University of East Anglia (UEA) with Anglia Ruskin University (Cossar et al, 2013).

The research included interviews with young people who were identified as vulnerable and at risk of abuse but were not currently involved with child protection services. While only young people over 11 years were interviewed, the findings have relevance for younger children too. The range of research methods, including a literature review, website analysis, focus groups and interviews, led to the design of a new conceptual framework which we believe will be of value to practitioners. Young researchers and advisors, all with experience or knowledge of the topic, were involved from the outset and played a key part in developing the research messages.

Recognition

There are few studies that examine how children think about abuse. Those that do so indicate confusion about whether the abuse is 'normal' and suggest that of all types of maltreatment, children are least likely to understand neglect as abusive. The study by Cossar and colleagues identified the obstacles their experiences as abusive, including confusion about the boundaries between physical abuse and punishment and about 'touch'. The internet forum analysis found that young people had difficulty in acknowledging that their parent could be abusive and were confused when a parent behaved unpredictably. They might feel they deserved their treatment and might blame themselves, particularly where sexual abuse involved coercion through grooming or psychological pressure.

—

One young person using a helpline commented:

> "I'd brush it off; or sort of think two things at the same time…? Like on the one hand this is wrong and on the other, main side, no, I deserve it, they're just angry, I shouldn't be so bad, it's not so bad." (Cossar et al, 2013, p 37)

From the interviews with the young people it was found that recognising abuse was more straightforward when it applied to someone else rather than to their own situation because of the complex emotions involved. Young people were able to reflect back on how hard it was for them to understand their experiences when they were small; now they were older, they could see how bad things had been. Recognition was likely to increase with age, with a gradual understanding born perhaps of more opportunities to compare their experiences with others. However, the study suggests that, at any particular time, a child's experience of thinking about abuse could be on a spectrum ranging from lack of recognition through partial recognition to clear recognition. With partial recognition, children had had a sense that something was wrong but were not sure whether it was enough of a problem to tell someone about or were unable to articulate the problem: "I think I was too young to realise, it was just I didn't like being there" (Cossar at al, 2013, p 63).

Even when recognition of abuse was clear, this did not always result in seeking help. Although much of the literature on disclosure depicts a linear process, with telling leading to help, the outcome of this research suggests a more complex picture, which requires us to take a step back and to be aware of the challenges for a child in interpreting their own experience. A helpful person might start this process of understanding through conversation. The researchers identified this as 'dialogic recognition'. One young person was helped by a good friend: "I kind of woke up and I realised, what the hell am I doing?" (Cossar et al, 2013, p 63).

For some young people, recognition can come very much later, when supportive relationships and a safe environment make it possible for them to reflect back and understand things differently. This is an argument for providing help at a later stage when recognition has been made possible as a result of adult support.

Several young people in this study had been identified as at risk from exploitation in relationships with peers but had not considered themselves to be at risk. Reports from the OCC inquiry into sexual exploitation in gangs and groups illustrate the realities for young people dealing with sexual violence (Beckett, 2013; Berelowitz et al, 2013). Young women and, less often, young men in a controlling relationship or gang situation may experience sexual violence that they do not construe as abusive. The reports identified resignation and self-blame, even for rape, in the context of young people accepting gendered stereotypes. Consent and coercion are 'slippery concepts' requiring discussion and improved understanding between young people (Coy et al, 2013, p 11). Given recent research on the high level of abuse in peer relationships, an understanding of the barriers to young people's recognition of abuse is essential to their protection (Barter et al, 2009).

Telling – and the importance of not relying on verbal disclosure

The Recognition and Telling study identified further barriers to 'telling' about abuse. The five main ones identified in the website analysis were: an emotional barrier such as shame; worry about the family knowing and family loyalty; thinking the problems were not sufficiently serious; threats from the abuser; and fear of not being believed. Emotional barriers to telling were most frequently mentioned in this part of the study. Even finding the words might be hard, as is shown by a statement from a young woman who had tried to talk about being raped as a young girl: "… for some strange reasons whenever I try to tell someone about the abuse I suffered, I get muscle spasms to my jaw and I end up giving up" (Cossar et al, 2013, p 41).

The study drew out from the interviews a continuum of telling: at one end, not telling and remaining 'hidden', where a child may actively avoid telling or passively not do so, and, at the other end, telling with the purpose of seeking help. In between is the trigger point of 'signs and symptoms' and 'prompted telling' (see Figure 5.1).

Hidden and active avoidance of telling

This encompassed loyalty and fear:

> "it's hard to tell on people you love" (Cossar et al, 2013, p 67)

> "When I was younger, my mum always told us they are not to be trusted ... so we told them, no my mum and dad weren't hitting us, nothing is wrong.... Mum told him [little brother] if he says the truth that they are going to take me and my brother away." (Cossar et al, 2013, p 67)

> "I really really wanted to open my mouth and just tell them everything and just get out of there but I knew that I would have to go back to my mum on that night and then she would have definitely heard about that and I would have had a bad experience and I had a massive fear of that, so I dared not mention anything." (Cossar et al, 2013, p 67)

Previous negative experiences of help could be a barrier: one young person's negative experience of foster care led him to say: "I would rather stay with me mum no matter what the consequences" (Cossar et al, 2013, p 67).

An immediately supportive response from an adult to a child's attempts to tell mattered greatly, both in terms of effective immediate help and longer-term benefit.

Passively not telling

This includes the situation of a young person who may recognise abuse but not feel able to tell anyone. One young person said that if someone had asked her what was wrong, she would have told them, but no one did.

Signs and symptoms

Recognition by an adult was conceptualised as 'telling' of a different kind. In this study, most young people's problems were picked up through signs and symptoms and not by young people talking about abuse. So, while their behaviour and demeanour brought them to the attention of services, their underlying needs were not always understood. The research suggests that if a young person feels they are being blamed for being the problem because of their troublesome behaviour, they may not believe they will be listened to, and this becomes a barrier to both recognition and telling about the underlying abuse.

Prompted telling

A sensitive and persistent response from a trusted person to indications that not all is well matters greatly: young people described how this could prompt recognition of their own situation, which could progress to telling and getting help. One young woman related her experience with a trusted teacher:

> "I was upset that past week and she asked me how I had been since the one before and I said I had been fine and Miss said, 'Well that is not completely true because the last week has not been so good as it could have been' and then I just started crying and she asked what was wrong and I said that I couldn't tell her. Then everyone else went and she stayed and she said, 'You can always tell me anything because you normally do, so whenever you are ready just go for it.'" (Cossar, 2013, p 70)

This young person was then able to disclose that she had been raped by showing the teacher her diary where she had recorded it, having been unable to tell anyone for a year.

Purposeful telling

Actively telling someone was often dependent on having a trusted person and also relied on their accessibility and ability to act. The barriers to telling noted earlier came into play again in shaping the way in which young people decided to tell, with several comments on the merits of putting experiences down in writing.

How children manage telling

It was clear from the study that children and young people actively manage the process by choosing whom to tell and by weighing up the consequences. Young people interviewed linked their motive for telling to the type of person they would choose to tell. To stop the abuse, they would choose a police officer, social worker or teacher. This confirmed the information from the website analysis, where professionals had the highest mention of those who were told; however, in only 42% of cases was it clear that anyone had been told. When young people were advising others, they most frequently suggested telling a professional – the highest recommendation being to tell a teacher.

If the motive for telling was emotional support, the indications from the interviews were that friends were more likely to be told. However, telling friends was not straightforward. While they may provide emotional support, they might not be trustworthy, and young people chose carefully. This is particularly relevant where peer abuse is involved.

Emotional factors in telling were powerful: as well as acting as a barrier, these could sometimes overwhelm the rational process. This would lead to purposeful telling but one that the researchers described as 'precipitated'. A young person who had endured abuse from her stepfather for some time only reported it when she felt she had to speak to somebody "because it was just killing me" (Cossar, 2013, p 71). A sensitive, encouraging response to young people who try to tell and are finding it hard is essential and can take time: 'telling that is tentative, delayed or uncertain should not be viewed as a sign that the young person is not credible' (Cossar et al, 2013, p 113).

Figure 5.1 represents the conceptual framework drawn from the research and can be used to make sense of an individual child's past or present pathway: this will not be linear and may include some 'dead ends' (Cossar et al, 2013, pp 103–9). Using it in work with a young person can assist an understanding of their own experience.

Figure 5.1: Framework for understanding recognition, telling and help

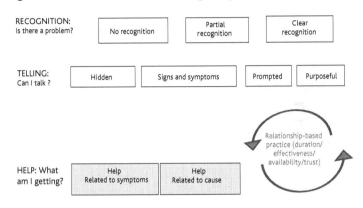

Help

The main themes to emerge from the study concerned the qualities of helpers and trusting, enduring relationships. Not being judged, being believed and having helpers with knowledge or expertise who were accessible and available were all valued by young people. How information about them was passed on counted towards the development and maintenance of trust, as did a sense of really being cared for:

> "As I got to know her then I started to trust her and things like that and then I started talking to her, it is now a lot easier to tell her my problems." (Cossar, 2013, p 75)

Some important themes emerged about help in relation to recognition and telling:

—

- Help might precede recognition, as with a supportive and understanding response to signs and symptoms.
- Adult responses influenced future access to and use of help. A poor experience had a negative impact on young people's recognition and telling about subsequent needs, while a good experience of help could result in a 'virtuous circle' such that the young person might be more likely to access help with future difficulties (see Figure 5.1).
- Help might be needed later, when recognition comes after safety is gained. This has particular relevance to children in care or those adopted from care who may not be able to fully use help until they are safely placed and may have a recurring need for support at different life stages.

Confidentiality

One aspect of the research was to find out if the desire for confidentiality might be a key barrier to young people telling or asking for help and whether professionals thought there was any 'space' for consideration of the right way to manage a disclosure. Discussions with professionals indicated that they felt they had very little leeway, even when managing the timing of passing on information might be in the interests of a young person.

When the researchers examined young people's use of the internet forum, the desire for confidentiality did not appear to be a barrier to telling or recommending others to tell. The interviews did uncover concerns about loss of trust through a breach of confidence and that the fear of information being passed on would prevent some children from talking. However, a minority of young people in this study thought that information should never be passed on without consent. The most important point to emerge was not that young people thought that secrecy was wanted or expected, but that the response following their disclosure was what mattered most. It was important to them that helping adults discussed their proposed actions with them, were clear about sharing information and showed their concern by doing this, leading to greater trust in the long term.

"At the time when I spoke to her about that I felt a bit uncomfortable talking to her about things ... because she told me that she had done it, she was also worried about me, just knowing that she was like worried about me ... it just made me feel like I could talk to her about pretty much anything." (Cossar et al, 2013, p 78)

As has been described, many young people actively make decisions about who and how to tell, and on telling, their expectations are that action will be taken. However, we cannot be sure how much of a barrier the desire for confidentiality is, given how long it took some young people to tell and how fears of the consequences could often be borne out. It would help if young people could know beforehand how a disclosure would be managed. For them, above all, to be believed and supported is essential. Professionals need to exert careful judgement when managing the process in the interests of the individual young person. Child-centred practice means going at their pace wherever possible, engaging with them in plans about their protection, taking their fears seriously, building trust and being open about what will happen.

Children living with parental alcohol misuse

While there has been considerable research on the impact of parental *substance* misuse on children, there are many gaps in our knowledge of the specific impact of parental *alcohol* misuse and of help from children's perspectives. The OCC therefore commissioned a literature review of both topics and the findings were discussed with young people with experience of parental alcohol misuse, who, since this is still very much a hidden problem, suggested the title, *Silent voices* (Adamson and Templeton, 2102).

It is known that many more children are affected by parental alcohol misuse than come to the attention of services, including services for children 'in need', and that alcohol misuse features prominently in cases of high risk. However, the impact on children of different levels of consumption by parents is not well understood and the potential for harm cannot be assumed to be limited to those with a particular pattern of alcohol misuse. The problems are ones about which children and families may remain silent for many years. The study identified the public perception of the acceptability of alcohol, and the consequent difficulty in identifying their own need for help, as a major barrier for young people.

Many children live not only with their parents' alcohol misuse but also with accompanying family conflict and with violence. Children live with the tension of wanting people to know and being fearful of that exposure; they experience isolation, loss and anxiety; they may be neglected; they take on overburdening responsibilities for the care of their parents and the household; and they may suffer educationally or emotionally from the inaccessibility and unreliability of the parent. Yet, many remain loyal and loving to parents regardless. We found, too, that young people who had good support could emerge strengthened. However, this growth in resilience should not be confused with the kind of coping mechanisms in evidence as young people struggled to 'get by' from day to day, some of which were harmful to their well-being.

Recognition

Young people who were part of a support group reflected:

> "Some children are uncertain of what 'it' [the problem] is and so they do not know what to talk about or who to talk to." (Adamson and Templeton, 2012, p 26)

Adult denial and secrecy

Many parents do not see their excessive drinking as a problem nor understand the impact on their children:

> "I won't tell anyone but I write in my notebook and show it to my social worker. My parents found my book and they were so angry they said I had let them down by writing it for everyone to read." (Adamson and Templeton, 2012, p 25)

One of the studies referenced in the review provided this message from young people to their parents: "Realise that the denial and the hiding makes it more difficult for me to trust them but also to trust other people" (Adamson and Templeton, 2012, p 64; quoting from Bernays et al, 2011).

Living with the consequences of a parent's problem drinking was found to be stigmatising. Young people were also acutely conscious of a wider denial of the problems of alcohol use and that drinking is promoted as a fun activity.

Finding the words

Some children may feel overburdened, perhaps having lived with their parents' alcohol misuse for many years, and do not know how to talk about it. In the view of the young contributors to this study, children do not want to be pushed into talking but need to know that support is available: "It's got to be the child's decision to speak but we need to let them know it's okay to speak" (Adamson and Templeton, 2012, p 28).

The research overview found:

> It can be very hard for children to talk about what is going on. Children need time to develop a relationship of trust and to feel safe; they also need to understand confidentiality and what will happen with the information they share with others.' (Adamson and Templeton, 2012, p 65)

Daily life

> "My brother who is ten says he wants to end it all, my mum also says she wants to die. She really needs to talk to someone but there is no one? I am not getting any sleep. I am scared what I will find when I wake up or what might happen whilst I am sleeping." (Adamson and Templeton, 2012, p 30)

Children had to find ways of coping, and this could mask their problems: "Even though I was having them problems at home I didn't let them show in school" (Adamson and Templeton, 2012, p 57; quoting from Bernays et al, 2011).

Help

Children described the need to escape and have safe places to go. They would turn to neighbours and friends for respite but it was not always possible to find somewhere safe: "I need somewhere safe to go quickly when mum starts drinking and cutting herself but where can I go?" (Adamson and Templeton 2012, p 24).

One 10-year-old said: "I wish we had somewhere safe where we can go to quickly until things are better at home" (Adamson and Templeton 2012, p 21).

Friends could help but there were limits: "It's good to have friends to talk to but you can't always talk to friends about your problems and they can't always be around"(Adamson and Templeton, 2012, p 21). However, peer support, particularly in groups, did assist in providing relief. The chance to have fun as well as get support was very important. Young people did not want to be seen as victims: 'Children do not want to have an identity that is based on being the "child of an alcoholic"; they want to be viewed as more than this' (Adamson and Templeton, 2012, p 26).

Being able to talk with someone when they needed to and to be heard were the most important kinds of support children and young people wanted, together with a trusting relationship with a professional who really understood their needs.

The study shows how important it is to consider the child's individual experience of living with problem drinking and to look at the impact on them. This needs to happen whether or not the alcohol misuse accompanies domestic violence or mental ill health: there are issues for children that are specific to parental alcohol misuse. For the child, barriers to support are exacerbated by denial in their family and by society at large.

Understanding the problem from the child's perspective cuts through the problems of defining the differential impact of binge, problem and dependent drinking and gets to the heart of the matter: how children are affected by their parents' alcohol consumption and how they can get support that will make a difference to their lives.

What does child-centred practice mean for children and young people?

As this chapter was being written, serious case reviews (SCRs) following the deaths of young children provoked questions about the extent to which children are seen or heard despite many earlier alerts that adequate child protection requires such actions. The review of Daniel Pelka's death indicated that no one really tried to talk with him, listen to him or understand his experience. Hamzah Khan's sibling told police about the home situation but follow-up action was apparently not pursued by children's services. It continues to be the case that vulnerable children are too often not seen or heard and remain invisible.

The research discussed here confirms that children may 'tell' about needs and abuse in a variety of ways. So, while it is vital to see and engage with them, it is also important not to rely on children talking about abuse and to understand why it might be hard for them to talk about difficult experiences. To rely unduly on a child's own recognition of their needs, or their ability to talk about abuse as the first step on the way to help, is to place too much responsibility on them for their own protection. Children need adults to be vigilant and to provide a safe environment in which telling and help become more possible. Adults need to understand the signs that might indicate abuse or need, and offer support without making assumptions about either 'difficult' or 'coping' behaviour.

Children's rights to protection are not respected if their denials that abuse is occurring are given more weight than non-verbal evidence to the contrary. If children do not talk about abuse or deny that it is taking place but there are still grounds for concern, evidence suggests that practitioners should work at establishing a trusting relationship in order to understand what is troubling them and to help them.

There is a consistency in the messages children and young people have conveyed to us through the research described here and in other recent work from the Children's Commissioner on safeguarding and protection (Berelowitz et al, 2013; Lefevre et al, 2013). The value placed on access to trusting relationships with caring adults who are interested in them as individuals and will 'stick with' them has come across clearly, as have the obstacles in children's journeys to help.

We need to help children and young people to feel more able to ask directly for help. It is essential to make clear to children and young people what they can expect and rely on in response to telling an adult. There are good examples of children's involvement in developing relevant information for other children and in giving feedback on help. Respecting their right to be heard means giving children a voice that makes a difference. Respecting their right to protection means acting on what they are telling us.

References

Adamson, J. and Templeton, L. (2012) *Silent voices: supporting children and young people affected by parental alcohol misuse*, London: OCC. Available at: www.childrenscommissioner.gov.uk

Allnock, D. and Miller, P. (2013) *No one noticed, no one heard: a study of disclosures of childhood abuse*, London: NSPCC.

Barter, C., McCarry, M., Berridge, D. and Evans, K. (2009) P'artner exploitation and violence in teenage intimate relationships'. Available at: www.nspcc.org.uk/inform

Beckett, H., with Brodie, I., Factor, F., Melrose, M., Pearce, J., Pitts, J., Shuker, L. and Warrington, C. (2013) *'It's wrong ... but you get used to it'. A qualitative study of gang-associated sexual violence towards, and exploitation of, young people in England*. London: OCC. Available at: www.childrenscommissioner.gov.uk

Berelowitz, S., Clifton, J., Firmin, C., Gulyurtlu, S. and Edwards, G. (2013) *'If only someone had listened'. Final report of the inquiry into child sexual abuse in gangs and groups*, London: OCC. Available at: www. childrenscommissioner.gov.uk

Bernays, S., Houmoller, K., Rhodes, T. and Wilson, S. (2011) *See me, not just the problem: hiding, telling and coping with a difficult life*, London: London School of Hygiene and Tropical Medicine.

Clifton, J. (2012) 'The child's voice in the child protection system', in M. Blyth and E. Solomon (eds) *Effective safeguarding for children and young people: what next after Munro?*, Bristol: The Policy Press.

Cossar, J., Brandon, M., Bailey, S., Belderson, P., Biggart, L. and Sharpe, D. (2013) *'It takes a lot to build trust'. Recognition and Telling: developing earlier routes to help for children and young people*, London: OCC.

Coy, M., Kelly, L., Elvines, F., Garner, M. and Kanyeredzi, A. (2013) *'Sex without consent, I suppose that is rape'. How young people in England understand sexual consent*, London: OCC.

Lefevre, M., Burr, R., Boddy, J. and Rosenthal, R. (2013) *Feeling safe, keeping safe: good practice in safeguarding and child protection in secondary schools*, London: OCC.

Miens, E. (1997) *Security of attachment and the social development of cognition*, Hove: Psychology Press.

Munro, E. (2011) *The Munro review of child protection. Final report: a child-centred system*, London: The Stationery Office.

Munro, E. (2012) *The Munro review of child protection. Progress report: moving towards a child-centred system*, London: The Stationery Office. Available at: www.gov.uk/government/publications/progress-report-moving-towards-a-child-centred-system

Rees, G., Gorin, S., Jobe, A., Stein, M., Medforth, R. and Goswami, H. (2010) *Safeguarding young people: responding to young people aged 11 to 17 who are maltreated*, London: The Children's Society.

Schofield, G. (2008) 'Providing a secure base: an attachment perspective', in B. Luckock and M. Lefevre (eds) *Direct work; social work with children and young people in care'*, London, BAAF.

6

Responding to adolescent risk: continuing challenges

Leslie Hicks

Introduction

Many practitioners are concerned that the needs of adolescents may be less readily identifiable than those of more overtly dependent, younger children. While much practice for those involved in children's services consists of work with teenagers, challenges remain in identifying the risk of adolescent neglect and in responding to it effectively. This chapter examines the core areas that present obstacles to successful multi-agency practice in respect of understanding and addressing neglect in teenage years.

The vital importance of protecting and enabling younger children is indisputable. In line with a commitment to the well-being of all children, practitioners are keenly aware that adolescence represents a period in childhood when opportunities need to be maximised in order to reap later benefits in a well-rounded adulthood. This adolescent period of child development is well known for its challenges (Aldgate et al, 2005), not least in terms of children who are coming to grips with establishing a secure identity (Danielet al, 1999). It is thus perhaps unsurprising that children of all ages, including adolescents, are seen to be neglected. In England and Wales, neglect is the main initial reason for being the subject of a child protection plan, accounting for 41% in the year ending 31 March 2013 (Department for Education, 2013), with almost a quarter of all children between the ages of 10 and 15 years. In extreme cases, life is placed at risk, with approximately a quarter of all serious case reviews (SCRs) focusing on teenagers as victims, of whom 10% are aged 16 or over (Rees et al, 2011). As the chapter by Jenny Pearce in this book indicates, adolescents form the majority of those targeted by perpetrators of sexual abuse in recently reported cases of extensive child sexual exploitation. Clearly, the teenage years can be fraught with difficulties and neglect is likely to form part of the experience. The concerning issue is that adolescent neglect remains in danger of continuing to receive scant policy attention, with a corresponding lack of consolidation in practice and in research.

This chapter draws on a research project that was one of 11 studies in the government-funded Safeguarding Children Research Initiative (Davies and Ward, 2012). The research took as its focus the neglect of adolescents and explored this by means of a comprehensive literature review of extant research and policies (Stein et al, 2009) and a series of focus groups with young people (NSPCC, 2010) and with a broad range of multi-agency professionals working in children's services (Hicks and Stein, 2010). The project received ethical approval from the Institute of Research in the Social Sciences Ethics Committee at the University of York and was underpinned by two advisory groups. A full account of the research findings and processes, including the participatory nature of the project, can be found elsewhere (Rees et al, 2011).

The research highlighted the diverse range of systems through which neglected young people initially come to the attention of professionals: education, health and youth justice, as well as social care. The literature review emphasised the need for insight to be drawn together as part of a 'joined-up' approach to understanding neglect and that successful multi-agency working is a prerequisite for effectively meeting the needs of these young people. Fundamental to achieving success in these areas is the need for a re-examination of current definitions of neglect in respect of age-related distinctions and perspectives, along with the need for a fuller understanding of this area in order to inform adolescent-sensitive developments in practice, policy and research (Rees et al, 2011). Taken together, these areas are crucially important in the drive forward from the Munro review towards effective child protection policies and practices that are increasingly child-centred.

Reassuringly for those working with adolescents, the Munro review drew attention to distinctive issues relating to young people, including areas such as self-harm and sexual exploitation, highlighting the need for appropriately tailored interventions (Munro, 2011). The response from government was encouraging insofar as it confirmed overtly the need to offer help to teenagers (Department for Education, 2011a, 2011b). This degree of consensus is helpful, yet difficulties remain in achieving these aims. Three aspects representing potential blocks to progress arising from our research are discussed in this chapter. These include challenges in defining adolescent neglect, working across agencies and establishing successful working.

Challenges in defining and assessing adolescent neglect

An essential part of work in this area is achieving consistency and agreement in relation to what adolescent neglect entails. Age plays an important part in establishing what is determined as neglectful. For example, there are major differences between the adequacy of supervision for six year olds and that for those who are 16. At the level of policy, formal guidance in England and Wales provides a description of neglect that is applicable up to the age of 18 years, with related guidance on neglect highlighting distinctions in assessing well-being (HM Government, 2013). The literature review strand of our research revealed negligible discussion of definitions of adolescent neglect in research and policy arenas (Stein et al, 2009). Most usually, neglect is regarded as involving *omission*; however, for teenagers, there are likely to be important concerns relating to *commission*, such as being made to leave home by care-givers (Rees and Lee, 2005). Here, basic needs are overlooked and factors come into play that may include emotional, supervisory and physical neglect in combination.

In terms of research, both the definition and measurement of neglect lack consistency (Zuravin, 1999; Sedlak, 2001) and indicate a discrepancy between the views of professionals and those of young people, where the latter have a tendency towards being more accurate predictors of outcomes (Farmer and Lutman, 2010). Including the views of young people is crucially important to the successful assessment of neglect. What needs to be borne in mind here is that, for various reasons, young people may underestimate the extent to which they are being neglected. For example, young people often show a strong sense of privacy and loyalty to their families and are broadly accepting of their own parenting.

Identifying neglect is a complex task and never more so than in respect of adolescence. With increasing maturity, for adolescents, the boundaries between dependence and independence are seldom clearly defined. This life stage is one where views differ widely about the extent to which young people may be seen as dependent on adults, or as responsible for themselves. The age at which young people may legally behave in specific ways demonstrates the ambiguities that abound when a young person is regarded as 'sufficiently mature' and can be held responsible for their own actions. For example, there are differences in the ages at which a young person may consent to having sex, be held criminally responsible, sign a passport, enter a bar unaccompanied by an adult, leave school, donate blood, own a house – and more. Practitioners who participated in the qualitative stages of our research were keenly aware of the implications of these variations, since such equivocal norms prompt uncertainty in young people and in their parents or carers.

Chronologically or otherwise, the transition from childhood to independence and all that is entailed in this shift is not clearly determined. What is achieved by teenagers, and when this occurs, will depend on individual abilities, family context and wider cultural concerns. In this way, what constitutes neglect becomes a matter for individual judgement and needs to take into account the views of young people, families and carers, as well as professional vantage points. For example, a young person may wish to act autonomously, parents may turn the young person away from home and professionals may identify particular vulnerabilities and a need for support in the young person, who additionally may be showing signs of self-neglect. Further, different ages in adolescence may have different implications: for example, a young teenager struggling with sexual development and other identity issues may be contending with difficulties distinct from those experienced by an older teenager facing 'emergent adulthood'. Effective assessment of adolescent neglect needs to build on basic awareness of behaviours and self-care such that differing expectations of appropriateness are made explicit and taken into account when making decisions about providing support.

While individual situations are important, broader cultural contexts will influence the ways in which neglect is defined. This is likely to vary in the light of what is seen as acceptable in terms of standards of care. Parenting patterns vary considerably and practitioners often experience a lack of parental concern about adolescents:

> "The risk that we all are presented with is parents are less committed to teenagers ... frequently the referrals into our service [social care] are actually from the parents themselves, they're not from the schools who should be referring them in." (Professional's view)

Clearly, an emphasis on cultural factors should be included in the priority of promoting healthy child development and well-being, which needs to be kept in sight at all times.

Although work with adolescents may represent a considerable proportion of the caseload of children's services staff, the all-encompassing nature of this work is not always regarded as 'working with adolescent neglect'. This may result from the apparent normalisation of neglect, where this is viewed frequently as widespread in teenagers' lives. Equally, the general absence of vocabulary that positions neglect alongside adolescent experience may serve to compound such normalisation. Practitioners in our research noted the value of being able to use an appropriate vocabulary and categorisation, which made permissible the prioritisation of adolescents' needs as distinct from those of younger children.

As indicated already, for adolescents, neglect does not necessarily relate directly to omission of some form. Some acts of commission may be seen as neglectful or may contribute to young people being neglected, such as being abandoned by parents and carers, being ejected from the family home owing to changes in family structure, or being included in drug cultures. While neglect is often seen as persistent, both acute and chronic forms of neglect are important here. Correspondingly, distinctions between emotional abuse and neglect are not always easy to make; however, it is important to remember that these categorisations are of less concern than the consequences experienced by the young person.

Challenges in working with adolescent neglect across agencies

Sharing concern

Adolescent neglect is complex and varied in its origins and consequences, which means that it is unlikely that all attendant needs can be met by a single agency. Efficient and effective working relationships between professionals are required to prevent adolescents 'falling through the net' of potential gaps between services. Establishing these relationships assists in developing an understanding of agencies' statutory responsibilities, thresholds, procedures and policies, roles and capacities, all of which serve the purpose of enabling a successful working dynamic. Early intervention may serve to avoid a lead agency being identified. Nevertheless, recognition of the effect that neglect may have on specific lives becomes a matter for shared concern even where the threshold for multi-agency working is not reached.

Making assumptions explicit

Arriving at consistency in defining adolescent neglect lays the foundation for multi-agency working, where the identification of need is an essential preliminary to intervention. Professional judgements play a vital part here and staff are responsible for decisions that draw on contextual norms. These are rarely articulated within teams or across agencies. Staff taking part in our research were very keenly aware that assumptions about the circumstances of young people and about professional constraints and boundaries need to be made explicit in order to achieve agreement when making decisions. Clearly, establishing time and space for this exchange of viewpoints is fundamental to successful practice and to creating strong professional networks. Practitioners in our study noted the value of establishing frameworks and processes that aid communication and collaboration between professionals from different disciplines; they regarded the local safeguarding children board (LSCB) as offering one route towards the achievement of this.

Normalising neglect

Practitioners frequently encounter a general prevalence of 'low-level' adolescent neglect and, as noted previously, this contributes to an insidious normalising of neglect. This holds the potential to have an ongoing and corrosive effect on the well-being of young people, while never quite reaching accepted thresholds for intervention. This risk may be heightened owing to variation in the conceptualisation of neglect for different age groups of children and young people. Somewhat regrettably, this normalisation shapes the context for work. There are difficulties in making distinctions between what might be regarded as broadly acceptable within cultural contexts and neglect, which is likely to have extreme effects on the young person. Prioritisation of young people's health and development is seen to be helpful in retaining focus in these respects.

Engagement

The practitioners who took part in our study saw particular challenges with respect to engagement with adolescents. As autonomous behaviour increases and rights and responsibilities are learned, willingness either to accept the idea of needing support or to engage with professionals was seen to be difficult to achieve at times. Particular challenges emerge when setting this alongside practitioners' commitment to the important principles of enabling choice and consent for young people. Again, vocabulary was seen to be important here and although practitioners supported the growing need for independence in young people, many saw the phrase 'young person' as indicative of a level of responsibility for self that could be detrimental to well-being and that may obviate the accountability of others.

Added to the complexities surrounding engagement with young people is the parallel challenge of engagement with parents and carers.

Without this involvement, practitioners considered the possibility of working with the causes of neglect to be remote. Sympathetic to families whose experiences were complex, such lack of engagement was disturbing for practitioners, some of whom (eg Child and Adolescent Mental Health Service workers) tended not to proceed with work where parents or carers would not engage with their service: "If parents aren't on board then what's the point? It's a cycle of neglect; it feels like we sometimes reinforce it" (Professional's view). Given that neglect may consist of an accretion of experiences occurring over extended periods, it is often helpful to integrate knowledge about the past with present circumstances in order to inform the potential for change. Of course, there may be difficulties in managing full engagement owing to the level of resources available within an agency:

> "The tension arises in these things because there aren't enough people very often to do the long-term pieces of work in supporting these young people and indeed their families." (Professional's view)

Pragmatically, practitioners regarded working with parents or carers as well as the young person to be a high expectation, for example: "the parents hadn't been engaged for the last seven years so why should they [be] now?" (Professional's view).

Multi-agency working

Clearly, a multidisciplinary, shared approach to understanding and working with adolescent neglect offers a firm basis for good practice. Neglected young people may initially come to the attention of practitioners from a wide range of systems, including education, health, youth justice and social care. Practitioners themselves need to be engaged across agencies in order to keep pace with what is taking place, for/with whom and when. In addition to strategies that might promote team cohesion, such as joint training and clear guidelines and procedures (Anning et al, 2006), frameworks and processes to aid collaboration between professionals from different disciplines are vital.

Effectively meeting the needs of young people who are experiencing neglect or who are at risk of being neglected requires a high level of expertise. This includes communication skills, the appropriate sharing of information, an understanding of vocabularies and terminology, and robust supervision practices. The strength of these essential professional networks entails sustaining close working relationships, keeping pace with changes (eg in young people's circumstances), and the agreement of common goals.

Interventions

Our research showed that there are few studies that give insight into effective interventions in relation to adolescent neglect itself, as distinct from broader issues connected with maltreatment or with troubled adolescents. By widening our focus to include a greater range of research, our project identified a particular approach first noted by Hardiker et al (1991) and employed most recently by Davies and Ward (2012). Here, an ecological approach involving young people themselves underpins intervention, where the relationships between individual, family, community, cultural and structural dimensions are reflected in the three levels of interventions suggested in the model. These latter comprise primary, secondary and tertiary levels of intervention, each of which is summarised here (see Table 6.1) and described in detail elsewhere (Rees et al, 2011).

The primary level of intervention involves preventing the occurrence of neglect, and all services, as well as parents and carers, have a role to play here in engaging and promoting the health and well-being of adolescents. This level may involve a universal or targeted approach. Of particular importance is the general commitment of schools to the well-being of young people and to promoting citizenship, along with aspects of the personal, social and health education (PSHE) curriculum.

At the secondary level of prevention, involvement occurs as difficulties begin to emerge. Again, schools play an important part in noticing changes in a young person, such as their appearance deteriorating and becoming dishevelled. Where informal discussions with young people and parents yield no potential for engagement or change, an early assessment may be required in order to establish appropriate modes of formal intervention.

Where early intervention at secondary level is unsuccessful, tertiary interventions move beyond this towards the use of multifaceted approaches in order to prevent the reoccurrence of difficulties.

Table 6.1: Working with neglected adolescents

Primary prevention	Issues for practice
Schools and communities	Raising awareness of neglect by inclusion of neglect/adolescent neglect in PSHE curriculum. Providing opportunities for young people's involvement and participation. Range of extra-curricular activities and leisure opportunities
Parenting	The promotion of 'authoritative parenting', with a focus on supporting teenage development, eg through local parent groups
Secondary Intervention	Issues for practice
Early recognition of teenage neglect	Informal response, for example, meet and discuss with young person and parents (if appropriate). Seek early resolution to problems
If problems not resolved	Apply Common Assessment Framework – involve young person, meeting of staff from different agencies, identify lead professional and agree action
If problems persist or more severe	Application of Assessment Framework to understand impact of neglect on young person's health and development, decide on course of action, methods on intervention by which staff from respective agencies
Tertiary Intervention	Issues for practice
Ecological perspective	The research literature supports the use of multi-faceted interventions. Promoting the resilience of neglected young people by working with young people, parents, involving schools – and these can be reinforcing of each other
Specific evaluated interventions	These include Cognitive Behavioural Therapy (CBT) and Multi-systemic Therapy (MST) approaches – but generic programmes will need to be developed focusing on the specific developmental needs of neglected adolescents

Source: Hicks and Stein (2010, p 24)

Challenges to working successfully with adolescents who are neglected

Several obstacles stand in the way of bringing about successful working with neglected adolescents. The four major areas discussed here relate to risk, responsibilities, autonomy and knowledge.

The first challenging dimension for consideration here is that of risk itself. An essential preliminary to intervention lies in the referral for help. This is dependent on several factors, not least the practitioner's perception of risk in relation to age. Our research highlighted a concerning finding from international research studies in that professionals seemed likely to attribute blame to older adolescents when responding to vignettes about maltreatment. This tendency was accompanied by the perception that older young people were intrinsically less at risk by virtue of their age and were therefore less likely to be referred to agencies responsible for safeguarding and protection. There is a need to ensure that neglected adolescents do not become overlooked in the gaps between pathways arising from the Children Act 1989, in particular between section 47 – the 'duty to investigate' – and section 17 – 'children in need'.

A second obstacle to overcome, which relates closely to risk, is that of responsibilities. A relatively recent study by Rees et al (2010) echoes the previous findings in England, where, in line with other work on child neglect (Horwath, 2007), the perceptions of professionals in relation to potential maltreatment (as distinct from significant harm) were considerably influenced by the age of children. Older young people were thought to both influence maltreatment by their responses to it and to 'put themselves at risk', particularly by adopting particular behaviours locally when away from the home environment. Additionally, practitioners regarded older adolescents as being at lower long-term risk, especially in respect of emotional abuse and supervisory neglect. This was in part accounted for in terms of assumed resilience and the young person's capacity either to move away from risk-laden situations or to try to find help. Furthermore, practitioners anticipated several major potential barriers to making a referral, such as the likelihood of encountering high thresholds for intervention, pressure on resources, potential negative effects should a referral be unsuccessful and, very important, the problematic issue of attaining consent from young people. Of key concern here was the finding that by the age of 14 years, professionals considered referrals to be less likely to necessitate a child protection intervention. The extent to which this may be a self-fulfilling prophesy remains a matter for exploration.

Third, the issues of autonomy and concomitant choice for young people raise important concerns for professionals in terms of information sharing and taking action. While practitioners may feel that they need to share information or to act in the 'best interests' of a young person, the potential for alienation of young people runs high and without their participation and consent at every stage, young people may opt out of engagement. Working with neglected young people entails particular sensitivities in relation to establishing a balance between protection and participation. Developing a trusting relationship with young people is vital to sustaining effective practice in this area. Practitioners in our study identified the value of effective supervision to support this balance.

Taken together, the preceding issues raise important concerns about safeguarding, participation, older children and age. Key aspects here are the age at which young people are thought to be capable of 'standing on their own two feet' and the ways in which practitioners' assumptions about older young people, as distinct from the needs of young people, may drive referrals.

The fourth major challenge identified here relates to developing a stock of knowledge. An abiding aid to understanding the success of interventions lies in establishing a robust evidence base. Although the 'adolescent neglect' research has enabled recognition of an array of practice-based work taking place with vulnerable teenagers and their families, it is notable that little evaluative research exists in this field. This presents a major obstacle to developing consistently effective interventions. There are very few studies related to interventions that are targeted at young people aged 11–17 years. This means that there is an urgent need to establish an evaluative culture in agencies in order to capture what is taking place currently and to enable a better understanding of what neglect involves for adolescents and the ways in which difficulties may be externalised in order to develop robust, research-informed future interventions.

Implications for responding to risk in adolescence

Although there is cause for optimism about the direction of travel in relation to practice and adolescent neglect, much is still to be achieved. In the closing section of this chapter, consideration is given to the main areas for improvement in terms of practice, policy and research.

Key implications for practice

Practitioners' understanding of the risks involved for adolescents will be developed by an awareness of the existing evidence about the potential impact of neglect for this age group.

It is important to understand the views of young people when establishing the existence and severity of neglect, as they assist in understanding variations in the effects of particular family contexts and behaviours. Setting these alongside the external perspectives of practitioners will serve to strengthen the assessment of risk. While practitioners' assessments of neglect may vary, in England and Wales, the core assessment records contained in the assessment framework offer a set of age-specific indicators to support assessments and offer the potential to form a consistent method of defining neglect in relation to individual cases. For adolescents, the experience of neglect may be long-standing and practitioners may need to have an understanding of this in order to inform assessments of what is currently taking place. Broad assessments that take account of a range of experiences, such as being bullied or running away from home, will be helpful to understanding patterns of neglect. Distinctive contextual factors, such as caring for a parent or changes in family structure, may have particular effects on adolescents.

Practitioners may require flexibility in approach when working with young people in this age group to help with their involvement in working processes and to enable their autonomy and sense of self-respect. Having a practitioner identified with whom they can develop a consistent and trusting relationship will help to sustain engagement. Successful multi-agency practice requires a mutual understanding of assumptions made within and between agencies, as well as those made by young people and their parents or carers.

Conduits to enable clarity, for example in terms of definitions of adolescent neglect, what constitutes risk and differing thresholds between services, are essential here. Without a coherent, agreed definition, thresholds for intervention may prove to be problematic. While effective supervision is vitally important to good practice in general, given the complexities involved in working with the risk of adolescent neglect, supervision is a particularly important enabler.

Key implications for policy

A crucial finding from our research is that definitions of neglect vary according to the age of the young person. Drawing attention to some of the age-specific assessment issues contained in the core assessment records materials in relation to adolescence may go some way towards formulating more age-sensitive definitions of neglect.

Correspondingly, a greater degree of guidance on definitions may serve to develop more consistent and reliable data, for example in terms of age-sensitive child protection statistics. The 10–15-year age band includes primary school as well as early to mid-adolescence. Greater precision here would assist in understanding age-related child development issues related to the emergence of neglect in older age groups.

Given the importance of young people's viewpoints about neglect, offering a detailed emphasis on young people's experiences would form a useful aspect of policy guidance for practitioners.

Key implications for research

Perhaps unsurprisingly, all of the above present opportunities for research to fill in the gaps in knowledge that exist around the aetiology and consequences of adolescent neglect and potential responses to it. There is a pressing need to develop an evidence base in this area, which fits the UK context and uses a consistent approach related to frameworks and definitions derived from policy and practice. Importantly, although adolescent neglect is an area meriting specific focus, the relationship to other forms of maltreatment needs to be understood much more fully than data presently allow.

Conclusion

Crucial elements in the government's response to the Munro review place emphasis on a more informed view of risk and the development of a child-focused system, where social workers make better use of their professional judgements. These factors relate keenly to adolescent neglect, where, as this chapter has indicated, practitioners from different agencies need to share their understandings of what is involved in order to determine the needs of young people and to give centrality to their experiences. Emphasis on the development and support of social work expertise indicates that, in order to work more effectively, practitioners will need to increase their knowledge and skills such that the needs of adolescents can be addressed and interventions are appropriate to needs. Drawing on evidence-based approaches is essential. Approaches to working with adolescent neglect may need to be determined in relation to primary, secondary and tertiary interventions, and in accordance with the evolving experiences of young people. A focused understanding of these important elements is needed to inform policy and practice related to adolescents. The central challenge lies in achieving a shared concern for working with neglect and its effects on life chances for adolescents.

Acknowledgements
The research team was led by Mike Stein. Other members of the team included Gwyther Rees (The Children's Society) and Sarah Gorin (independent research consultant, formerly senior research officer, NSPCC). We valued assistance from former colleagues Jasmine Clayden (then University of York) and Sylvie Bovarnick (then NSPCC). The Department for Children, Schools and Families and the Department of Health commissioned the research and the project was supported by two project advisory groups. The advisory group of young people was hosted by NSPCC staff and the academic and policy group was chaired by Carolyn Davis. Appreciation and thanks go to all, particularly the young people and staff who took part generously in the empirical aspects of the study.

References

Aldgate, J., Jones, D., Rose, W. and Jeffery, C. (2005) *The developing world of the child*, London: Jessica Kingsley Publishers.

Anning, A., Cottrell, D., Frost, N., Green, J. and Robinson, M. (2006) *Developing multiprofessional teamwork for integrated children's services*, Maidenhead: Open University Press.

Daniel, B., Wassell, S. and Gilligan, R. (1999) *Child development for child care and protection workers*, London: Jessica Kingsley Publishers.

Davies, C. and Ward, H. (2012) *Safeguarding children across services: messages from research on identifying and responding to child maltreatment*, London: Jessica Kingsley Publishers.

Department for Education (2011a) *A child-centred system: the government's response to the Munro review of child protection*, London: DfE.

Department for Education (2011b) *Childhood neglect: improving outcomes for children: guidance for trainers*, London: DfE.

Department for Education (2013) *Characteristics of children in need in England: 2012 to 2013*, London: DfE.

Farmer, E. and Lutman, E. (2010) *Case management and outcomes for neglected children returned to their parents: a five-year follow-up study*, Research Briefing RB214, London: DCSF.

Hardiker, P., Exton, K. and Barker, M. (1991) 'The social policy contexts of prevention in child care', *British Journal of Social Work*, 21, 341–359.

Hicks, L. and Stein, M. (2010) *Neglect matters: a multi-agency guide for professionals working together on behalf of teenagers*, London: DCSF.

HM Government (2013) *Working together to safeguard children: a guide to inter-agency working to safeguard and promote the welfare of children*, London: DfE.

Horwath, J. (2007) *Child neglect: identification and assessment*, Basingstoke and New York: Palgrave Macmillan.

Munro, E. (2011) *The Munro review of child protection. Final report: a child-centred system*, Cm 8062, London: DfE.

NSPCC (National Society for the Prevention of Cruelty to Children) (2010) *Neglect matters, a guide for young people about neglect*, London: NSPCC. Available at: www.nspcc.org.uk/inform/publications/neglect_matters_wda70741.html (accessed 9 December 2013).

Rees, G. and Lee, J. (2005) *Still running II: findings from the second national survey of young runaways*, London: The Children's Society.

Rees, G., Gorin, S., Jobe, A., Stein, M., Medforth, R. and Goswami, H. (2010) *Safeguarding young people: responding to young people aged 11–17 who are maltreated*, executive summary, London: The Children's Society.

Rees, G., Stein, M., Hicks, L. and Gorin, S. (2011) *Adolescent neglect: research, policy and practice*, London: Jessica Kingsley Publishers.

Sedlak, A. (2001) *A history of the national incidence study of child abuse and neglect*, Rockville, MD: Westat Inc.

Stein, M., Rees, G., Hicks, L. and Gorin, S. (2009) *Neglected adolescents: literature review*, Research Brief DCSF-RBX-09-04, London: DCSF.

Zuravin, S.J. (1999) 'Child neglect: a review of definitions and measurement research', in H. Dubowitz (ed) *Neglected children: research, practice and policy*, Thousand Oaks, CA: Sage Publications, pp 24–46.

7

Moving on with Munro: child sexual exploitation within a child protection framework

Jenny J. Pearce

Introduction

This chapter argues for a conceptual shift in our understanding of child protection. Drawing on some of the key lessons from Munro's (2011) review of child protection, it argues that our understanding of child protection must develop from one focused on protecting younger children from abuse in the home to one incorporating the protection of older children from abuse located and experienced outside the home.

The chapter uses child sexual exploitation (CSE) as an example to illustrate the complexities of extending the child protection framework to embrace the needs of older children, particularly adolescents. It develops Munro's call for a systemic approach to understanding the difficulties faced by those working in child protection and her request for relationship-based thinking to inform the supervision of practitioners, helping them manage the anxieties that emerge when responding to difficult and emotive casework. It argues that future policy and practice to protect children from sexual exploitation should not only be modelled on reviews of recent cases where abusers have been prosecuted. Rather than using these reviews to blame individual practitioners for failing to recognise the exploitation of a child, it calls for a more nuanced understanding of the social context in which the practitioner is functioning. This is particularly relevant for practitioners understanding the social context in which a child's capacity to consent to sexual activity may be abused.

I argue that relationship-based child protection interventions with older children could be enhanced through learning action partnerships (LAPs). Originally developed by staff working with the Oak Foundation developing sustainable interventions to prevent child abuse, LAPs offer a model of engaging with young people as partners, recognising their capacity either to engage or disengage from the support and protection offered by children's services. LAPs provide us with a model for developing safeguarding with adolescents, who, unlike babies or toddlers, have the capacity to exert their own agency through taking safeguarding into their own hands, by 'going missing' or by rejecting support through other means.

In summary, the chapter moves through three stages. First, it notes that most discourses about 'child protection', including those addressed by the Munro review, have, in the main, overlooked the needs of vulnerable older teenagers who are being abused as they approach adulthood. Second, it draws on research with young people who have been sexually exploited to illustrate the multiple child protection needs that may be presented by older children. Third, it draws on some of the principles advocated in the Munro report to propose LAPs as a model for relationship-based engagement with young people as safeguarding partners. This relates to Munro's call for relationship-based interventions, suggesting a model of how these may be advanced with older young people in need of safeguarding and protection from abuse.

Recognising sexually exploited young people within a child protection framework

While there are excellent lessons to be learnt from Munro, many of which are outlined later, there is an overarching problem that needs to be addressed. The review, as with social work overall, has assumed that child protection means safeguarding younger children from abuse in their own homes (Jago et al, 2011; Pearce, 2013a). Munro notes:

> When the Secretary of State for Education commissioned this review of child protection in June 2010, a central question was 'what helps professionals make the best

judgments they can to protect a vulnerable child?'
(Munro, 2011, p 9)

This original question begs two further questions: what do we mean by 'vulnerable' and who is a 'child'? When considered through the lens of child protection policy, practice and training, we think of 'vulnerable' as pertaining to a child's exposure to danger in the home, usually danger from parents or carers, and a 'child' as being under 10 years old. Rarely is the vulnerability of the older young person embraced by child protection discourses (Rees et al, 2011, Warrington, 2013). Moreover, early intervention is assumed to be preventive work with the family during the 'early' years of a child's life rather than early intervention to embrace the needs of a teenager in transition to adulthood (Coleman, 2012).

The United Nations Convention on the Rights of the Child defines a child as anyone up to the age of 18 and outlines all children's right to protection from abuse and harm (United Nations, 1989). Research with older children has noted significant threats to their safety, which may emerge from sexual exploitation, peer-on-peer violence, gang-related violence and associated online abuse (Barter, 2009, 2011; Firmin, 2010, 2011). In the main, most of these threats occur outside, rather than inside, the home environment. Other forms of violence often experienced by older children connected to, though not necessarily perpetrated in, the family home arise through 'honour-based' violence and other gender-based domestic violence (Meetoo and Mirza, 2007; Sharpe, 2013). While some older children may welcome support to prevent, challenge and manage these threats, others may aggressively reject support, resisting it for fear of identification, the worry of family shame or 'dishonour', or through a lack of recognition of the abuse itself, alongside a desire to exercise choice and agency in decision-making about friends and relationships. The young person may retaliate with behaviour that labels them as 'offender' rather than 'victim', may actively avoid appointments, and may challenge or discard help from carers and parents. They may take action into their own hands with repeated episodes of 'going missing', episodes that invariably increase their vulnerability and take them further into the control of abusers

(Scott and Skidmore, 2006; Barnardo's, 2011; Beckett, 2011; Child Exploitation Online Protection Agency, 2011; Hackett, 2011). While the young person is clearly a victim of abuse, they themselves may not perceive or understand this to be so and may 'choose' to reject support that they feel they do not need, do not trust or do not understand.

It has been argued that the complexities facing children's services trying to identify and respond to these issues have not been incorporated into child protection training, are under-researched and are poorly developed (Berelowitz et al, 2013). Indeed, much of the focus in the Munro review is on dangers facing the 'child' (invariably assumed to be a young child) in the 'family' and on the anxieties facing practitioners trying to manage associated risks:

> First, abuse and neglect occur (although not exclusively) in the privacy of the family home so they are not readily identified ... there are difficult decisions to make about whether the parents can be helped to keep children safe from harm or whether the child needs to be removed. (Munro, 2011, pp 17–18)

Although it is acknowledged in this quotation that abuse and neglect are not exclusively experienced in the home, the 'difficult decisions' are seen to focus on whether or not to remove the child from home. In contrast, much of the research on the risks facing adolescents focuses on risks outside, rather than inside, the home environment. In the case of sexual exploitation, those who manipulate and abuse have an invested interest in drawing the child away from the home, separating them from family or carer support (Parents Against Child Sexual Exploitation, 2013). In cases of peer-on-peer violence and gang-associated sexual violence, adolescents may not confide in parents/carers or extended family members, who may themselves feel separated from threats outside their grasp or understanding. For example, a recent analysis of interviews and focus groups involving 188 young people living in gang-affected areas found that 65% of those who spoke of sexual violence had knowledge of sexually exploitative situations, 41% shared knowledge of incidents of individual perpetrator rape and 34% shared knowledge of multiple perpetrator rape. Despite this high level of knowledge of sexual violence, few understood the legal context or meaning of rape or sexual assault, and only one in 12 of these respondents said they expected young people to talk about this abuse. Those who would talk about it would talk to a peer rather than to a professional or family member (Beckett et al, 2013). Similar findings from other research about peer-on-peer sexual violence and teen dating violence show that the violence often implodes in peer groups away from the family or home setting, few young people will report or discuss the violence they experience with carers/parents, and many have little or confused understanding of the legal status of victims and perpetrators of violence (Firmin, 2011; Wood et al, 2011; Coy et al, 2013; Khan et al, 2013). In these situations, the 'difficult decisions' may not be about whether to remove the adolescent from home (although this is a possibility that cannot be excluded if cause for concern is linked to worries about familial abuse), but more about how to support parents/carers to identify and understand incidents of abuse taking place outside their home domain. It may also involve difficult decisions about the appropriateness of specific placements for young people who are placed in local authority care, or looked after. Once the abuse is recognised, further difficult decisions revolve around how to share information between the different professionals who should be involved in safeguarding adolescents and their peer groups, how to support families, carers and young people through the process of providing intelligence that could be used as evidence in a prosecution, and how to ensure that a multi-agency strategy holds the young people's welfare at heart.

Child sexual exploitation: a case study

To elaborate this point just a little further, I briefly draw on research from work with older teenagers affected by CSE. Until 2000, children 'involved in prostitution' could be prosecuted for soliciting offences, essentially penalised for behaviours that resulted from their abuse. In 2009, CSE was fully incorporated into the safeguarding children agenda, using the following definition:

Involves exploitative situations/contexts/relationships
where young people (or a third person or persons) receive
'something' ... as a result of performing, and/or others
performing on them, sexual activities. ... In all cases those
exploiting the child/young person have power over them
by virtue of their age, gender, intellect, physical strength
and/or economic or other resources. (Department for
Children, Schools and Families, 2009, p 9)

This definition, used in the Coalition government's *Tackling child
sexual exploitation action plan* (Department for Education, 2011), notes
the vulnerability of the child and the power of the abuser, guiding
policy and practice to focus attention on CSE as a child protection
issue. Despite this, the nature of the abuse is poorly understood
(Melrose and Pearce, 2013). Definitions continue to assume that the
perpetrator is an adult rather than embrace the possibility of a young
person being both and victim and a perpetrator (Firmin, 2013). We
still lack a comprehensive overview of the numbers affected and
the variety of forms of abuse experienced. A review by the Child
Exploitation Online Protection Centre (2011) noted information on
1,875 cases of 'localised grooming'. However, it identified problems
with its own limited definition of CSE and with reviewing the
different data recorded by police and children's services. The Office
of the Children's Commissioner (OCC) for England clarified that
data monitoring was inadequate, leaving gaps in our knowledge of
the extent and nature of CSE. Despite generic problems with data
monitoring, the OCC inquiry into CSE in gangs and groups noted
2,409 confirmed victims, and 16,500 cases recorded to be 'at risk'
of CSE over a 14-month period (Berelowitz et al, 2013). A review
of CSE in Northern Ireland noted it to be an issue of concern for
one in seven young people known to social services, with a further
one in five at significant risk (Beckett, 2011). These research findings
shows that, even with inadequate data-recording systems, evidence
of widespread abuse through CSE exists, with young people in their
teens being most at risk.

Research has shown that some factors increase teenagers'
vulnerability to CSE. A disproportionate number of young people

with learning difficulties are sexually exploited: a review of 461 cases showed 67 (15%) to have special educational needs (Jago et al, 2011). Although most identified victims are female, boys are also known to experience sexual exploitation (Lillywhite and Skidmore, 2006; Barnardo's, 2011; Beckett, 2011); and while recent media attention has suggested that CSE is a problem arising from the abuse of white girls by men of Pakistani origin, this is a limited picture, challenged by extensive research which shows that CSE can take place both within and across all communities (Barnardo's, 2011; Berelowitz et al, 2013; Melrose and Pearce; 2013). The dominance of the 'white girl' victim discourse has been challenged by the Muslim Women's Network review of 35 case studies from across England. This noted that Muslim young women could be affected by CSE: the majority of the victims in the study were between 13 and 14 years and the perpetrators were of Afghani, Bangladeshi, Indian, Pakistani, white and mixed heritage backgrounds. The review found that many of the victims of sexual exploitation in the study were being overlooked by front-line agencies and little, if anything, was being done to identify them (Muslim Women's Network, 2013).

Despite evidence from this and other research, our awareness of the need to protect older children from CSE is limited, with few local safeguarding children boards (LSCBs) having effective methods to protect young people and prosecute abusers (Jago et al, 2011). This is beginning to change as public awareness increases, cases are taken to court and perpetrators are prosecuted, and as inspectorates, such as the Office for Standards in Education (Ofsted), review LSCBs' progress in monitoring and responding to CSE. However, lessons from the Munro review warn us against an over-reliance on lessons from one-off Ofsted inspections or one-off serious case reviews. She warns against a sudden rush for a new policy or procedure as the cure for all ills, and against restricting our learning to findings from reviews that target failings in an individual without due acknowledgement of the failings of the whole system in which the individual works. Munro overtly calls for 'a move from a compliance to a learning culture' (Munro, 2011, p 5) and warns:

> Mechanisms for improvement have been pressure on
> professionals to try harder; reducing scope for individual
> judgment by adding procedures and rules; and increasing
> the level of monitoring to ensure compliance with them.
> (Munro, 2011, p 19)

These warnings against a culture of compliance and against an over-reliance on policy and procedure strategy documents are as applicable to developing interventions to work with CSE as they are to protecting younger children from abuse in the home. In a review of practitioners' responses to trafficked young people, many of whom were trafficked for sexual exploitation, it was noted that some of the excellent policies developed to offer referral routes and frameworks for good practice were ineffective without the support and supervision of staff. The impact of the extent of abuse uncovered by workers, the fast turnover of staff and the pessimism that little could be done to protect the child meant that few practitioners had confidence in the effectiveness of a written procedure without care of staff and supervision of their work (Pearce et al, 2013). Similar findings emerged from a review of LSCB interventions (Jago et al, 2011). Children who have been sexually exploited want to be trusted, want to be believed and want supported workers to stay with them throughout the process of identification, engagement and eventual prosecution of the abuser. The following quotes are from two different young women from recent research on CSE in gang-affected neighbourhoods. The first suggests why young women may not disclose their experience of abuse, and the second suggests why young people may not trust adults (professionals) to protect them:

> "She'll be scared, they will make her not even wanna
> speak again … she wouldn't be able to tell no one, it will
> be that bad." (Young woman, aged 15, quoted in Beckett
> et al, 2013, p 44)

And:

> "I got raped and when I finally spoke to the police about it they let him on bail and he came looking for me – why do they do that?" (Young woman, aged 17, quoted in Beckett et al, 2013, p 45)

The arguments presented earlier suggest that child protection frameworks have overlooked the needs of sexually exploited children and young people, who may be assumed to be exerting choice and agency (thus perceived to be choosing a relationship that might, by default, be exploitative) or who either passively or aggressively can reject support and/or take actions into their own hands and 'go missing'. Practitioners may not be trained to identify the abuse experienced by a young person as a result of CSE and may not feel equipped, supported or resourced to address the emerging problems. These and other factors contribute to child protection failing older exploited children, particularly those aged between 16 and 18, who are legally able to consent to sexual activity and who are in transition towards adulthood. Research on cases of CSE and reviews of children's experiences of taking a case through court to prosecute abusers suggest that many victims are distrusted, disbelieved and assumed to hold some responsibility for the abuse they have received (Berelowitz et al, 2013). I have proposed elsewhere that a 'social model' for understanding why children may consent to their own abuse is needed (Pearce, 2013b). I have argued that our dependence on Fraser guidelines and Gillick competences have led to the assessment of a child's ability to consent to sexual activity to depend on their capacity to understand and use contraceptives. This individual approach in a 'medical model' for thinking about consent to sexual activity restricts our understanding of the social pressures on the child to consent. Instead, I have argued that we need to develop a 'social model' of contextualising consent, one that addresses: the impact of being groomed for sexual exploitation; the impact of 'normalisation' of sexual violence between young people; the impact of poverty as a driver for 'survival sex' and the selling or swapping of sex for money, drugs or other benefits; and the impact of what I have called 'condoned consent' – an overarching culture in professional discourse that some young people will choose a lifestyle that includes violence and abuse (Pearce, 2013b). More work is needed to fully understand these social pressures, which can be experienced independently or converge, resulting in the young person consenting to their own sexual exploitation. This is just one component to be incorporated in relationship-based engagement with young people as safeguarding partners in the child protection system.

Moving on from having identified CSE as a case study to illustrate some of the complexities involved in developing appropriate child protection interventions with adolescents, I outline in the following section some early considerations of what relationship-based engagement with young people as safeguarding partners may look like.

Learning action partnerships as a framework for relationship-based engagement with young people as safeguarding partners in the child protection system

I argued earlier that our child protection systems have been dominated by assumptions that the child (usually considered to be less than 10 years old) is at risk of abuse within the home. I have noted that this limits our efforts to identify, research and evaluate methods of engaging with older children who may be abused outside the home. While we might appreciate that child protection interventions with an older young person (particularly those aged 16–18) will be different from those with a baby or a young toddler, we are unfamiliar with how to engage with them to support them away from violence and abuse. Although managing child protection procedures for any young person is complex, adapting a system that has essentially been designed to protect younger children abused in the home to become one that is capable of engaging with older teenagers who may be abused outside the home presents us with unexplored challenges.

I have also argued that although some of the Munro review colludes with this specific failing, there are important generic messages to learn from her work. Munro argues that good practice is relationship-based: when the relationship between practitioner and client is prioritised, a genuine engagement with and understanding of the problems can emerge. To make this effective, she strongly argues for social workers to be supported through ongoing supervision and support. While specific failings in an individual practitioner's work may occur, these are best identified and addressed through supervision. Reviews and inspections that focus only on individual failings or successes overshadow the importance of reviewing the generic system within which individual practice occurs. Taking some of these lessons to address how older children may be supported through the child protection system, I describe how LAPs may offer scope for practice that engages with young people to advance their protection from harm. The proposal outlined below is simply an attempt to start a discussion about what engaging with older young people through safeguarding relationships might look like. Many similar arguments were proposed as a result of reviews of good practice undertaken in the OCC inquiry (Berelowitz et al, 2013), which advocates a 'See Me, Hear Me' framework for engaging with children at risk of abuse. The overarching principle underpinning lessons from Munro and from research on CSE is that the relationship with the child or young person is of paramount importance.

The application of a LAP as a means to develop a relationship with a young person in need of protecting has originated from preventative work with communities who have experienced disadvantage and discrimination (for more details, see the Oak Foundation: www.oakfnd.org). There are some generic principles behind LAPs. Partners come together with the understanding that, although they each hold separate and different bodies of knowledge, neither is privileged over the other. The partnership recognises that individuals in a relationship will be influenced by external pressures such as job roles and responsibilities, home environments, financial constraints and social and economic opportunities. The relationship that builds between the partners will depend on individuals' understanding of the opportunities and constraints that each bring. The partners will agree to work together in order to learn from each other, giving time to find out about the others' perspectives, skills, interests and objectives. Finally, the partnership, underpinned by shared learning, will produce agreed action. While LAPs have historically been used as a framework to underpin sustainable community development, I am interested to see whether they might help approaches to engaging with young people in the child protection system. In summary, the principles behind LAPs are that partnerships are formed for learning and that partners develop agreed action to create change. This combination of learning, action and partnership is the foundation for developing sustainable interventions. I elaborate further on how this might inform the development of safeguarding relationships between young people and child protection practitioners in the following section.

Learning

The practitioner and the young person recognise that they can learn from each other. The practitioner recognises that they need to learn about the young person's experience of abuse: on- or offline, peer-on-peer, gang-affected, or linked to status, love and experimentation. The young person recognises that they need to learn about what the practitioner can offer them: a non-abusive relationship with resources that may help the process of making informed decisions about a safer future. Through this relationship, the young person may recognise some of their own strengths and learn how to manage their feelings differently. Through the development of a non-abusive and supporting learning partnership, they may begin to realise that the sexual activity they thought they were consenting to is actually abusive. This learning relationship continues over time and, with enhanced sharing of information, focuses more and more on how the young person can play an active role in protecting themselves from further abuse.

Action

The young person and the practitioner agree small actions, each linked to developing change. The change for the practitioner emerges as they increasingly understand the context in which the young person is experiencing abuse. The change for the young person emerges as they become more aware of their skills and experience, gaining confidence in accessing resources to leave abusive contexts.

Partnership

Recognising that the young person has agency, the practitioner approaches them to request the development of a working partnership. The partnership recognises that both the practitioner and the young person have important knowledge and skills but that each are working under specific constraints, as well as having the ability to develop particular opportunities. It recognises that the young person has the capacity to engage with or to leave the support offered by the practitioner and that the young person is functioning with influence from peers, family and others in their lives. The partnership provides the foundation for the relationship between the young person and the practitioner. It needs continual review to check that it is based on recognition of the different attributes brought to the partnership by each individual.

Conclusion

If we are seriously engaged in a review of child protection, we must address how we can protect older children from abuse they may experience outside the home. The three components of a LAP identified earlier may offer a way to approach a young person who is at risk of, or experiencing, abuse or exploitation. They are based on the importance of shared knowledge, on the recognition of different strengths and resources brought to the partnership, and on an understanding that change and action will happen through relationship-based partnership work. They require each partner to recognise that the other has a voice and can exercise agency. As such, the LAP may provide a foundation for engaging with child protection issues with older young people. While there are obviously many questions to identify and address, the LAP provides a starting point for discussion about how to engage with older children who have been abused and who will make the decision about who to talk to and when. I quote from a practitioner interviewed about her work with exploited and abused young people:

> "it's getting away from the concept of reporting, because
> it's not reporting. It's a process through a relationship

where you meet people over a period of time and they will incrementally tell a little bit more to one trusted person, whilst being able to retain some control over their information and what happens." (Professional in focus group B, quoted in Beckett et al, 2013, p 49)

This practitioner recognises the need for partnership with the young person, the need for time to allow the young person to develop trust and confidence, and the need for the young person to hold onto some control over their actions. These points echo some of the lessons we have learnt from Munro about the need for relationship-based interventions and the need for support and supervision for staff engaged with difficult and demanding child protection cases. Through developing relationships with and learning from young people who have experienced abuse, we can gain a better understanding of the social pressures they experience to consent to abusive sexual activity. Through these relationships, and through listening to young people, we can adapt our current child protection procedures to better safeguard older children as they approach adulthood.

References

Barnardo's (2011) 'Puppet on a string: the urgent need to cut children free from sexual exploitation'. Available at: www.barnardos.org.uk

Barter, C. (2009) 'In the name of love: partner abuse and violence in teenage relationships', *British Journal of Social Work*, 39(2), 211-233.

Beckett, H. (2011) *Not a world away: the sexual exploitation of children and young people in Northern Ireland*, Belfast: Barnardo's.

Beckett, H., Brodie, I., Factor, F., Melrose, M., Pearce, J., Pitts, J., Shuker, L. and Warrington, C. (2013) *'It's wrong but you get used to it'. A qualitative study of gang-associated sexual violence towards, and sexual exploitation of young people in England*, Luton: University of Bedfordshire.

Berelowitz, S., Clifton, C., Firmin, C., Gulyurtlu, S. and Edwards G. (2013) *'If only someone had listened'. Final report of the inquiry into child sexual exploitation in gangs and groups*, London: OCC.

Child Exploitation Online Protection Agency (2011) *Out of mind, out of sight: breaking down the barriers to understanding child sexual exploitation,* London: CEOP.

Coleman, J.C. (2012) *The nature of adolescence* (4th edn), London: Routledge.

Coy, M., Kelly, L., Elvines, F., Garner, M. and Kanyeredzi, A. (2013) *'Sex without consent, I suppose that is rape'. A report commissioned for the Office of the Children's Commissioner's inquiry into child sexual exploitation in gangs and groups,* London: London Metropolitan University.

Department for Children, Schools and Families (2009) *Safeguarding children and young people from sexual exploitation.* Supplementary guidance to *Working together to safeguard children,* London: HMSO.

Department for Education (2011) *Tackling child sexual exploitation: action plan,* London: HMSO.

Firmin, C. (2010) *The female voice in violence project: a study into the impact of serious youth and gang violence on women and girls,* London: ROTA.

Firmin, C. (2011) *This is it: this is my life: female voice in violence. Final report on the impact of serious youth violence and criminal gangs on women and girls across the country,* London: ROTA.

Firmin, C. (2013) 'Something old or something new: do pre-existing conceptualisations of abuse enable a sufficient response to abuse in young people's relationships and peer groups?', in M. Melrose and J. Pearce (eds) *Critical perspectives on child sexual exploitation and related trafficking,* Basingstoke: Palgrave Macmillan, pp 38–51.

Hackett, S. (2011) 'Harmful sexual behaviours', in C. Barter and D. Berridge (eds.) *Children behaving badly? Peer violence between children and young people,* West Sussex: Wiley-Blackwell.

Jago, S., Arocha, L., Brodie, I., Melrose, M., Pearce, J. and Warrington, C. (2011) *What's going on to safeguard children and young people from sexual exploitation? How local partnerships respond to child sexual exploitation,* Luton: University of Bedfordshire.

Khan, L., Brice, H., Saunders, A. and Plumtree, A. (2013) *A need to belong. What leads girls to join gangs,* London: Centre for Mental Health.

Lillywhite, R. and Skidmore, P. (2006) 'Boys are not sexually exploited? A challenge to practitioners', *Child Abuse Review*,15(5), 351–61.

Meetoo, V. and Mirza, H.S. (2007) 'Lives at risk: multiculturalism, young women and "honour" killings', in B. Thom, R. Sales, and J. Pearce (eds) *Growing up with risk*, Bristol: Policy Press.

Melrose, M. and Pearce, J. (eds) (2013) *Critical perspectives on child sexual exploitation and related trafficking*, Basingstoke: Palgrave Macmillan.

Munro, E. (2011) *The Munro review of child protection. Final report*, London: Department for Education.

Muslim Women's Network (2013) *Unheard voices: sexual exploitation of Asian girls and young women*, London: Muslim Women's Network. Available at: www.mwnuk.co.uk.

Parents Against Child Sexual Exploitation (PACE) (2013) 'Are parents in the picture?', Special report. Available at: www.paceuk.info.

Pearce, J.J. (2013a) 'What's going on to safeguard children and young people from child sexual exploitation? A review of local safeguarding children boards' work to protect children from sexual exploitation', *Child Abuse Review*, 21 June, doi: 10.1002/car.2269.

Pearce, J.J. (2013b) 'Contextualising consent', in M. Melrose and J. Pearce (eds) *Critical perspectives on child sexual exploitation and related trafficking*, Basingstoke: Palgrave Macmillan, pp 52–68.

Pearce, J.J., Hynes, P. and Bovarnick, S. (2013) *Trafficked young people: breaking the wall of silence*, London: Routledge Falmer.

Rees, G., Hicks, L., Gorin, S. and Stein, M. (2011) *Adolescent neglect: research, policy and practice*, London: Jessica Kingsley Publishers.

Scott, S. and Skidmore, P. (2006) *Reducing the risk: Barnardo's support for sexually exploited young people*, London: Barnardo's.

Sharpe, N. (2013) 'Missing from discourse: South Asian young women and sexual exploitation', in M. Melrose and J. Pearce (eds) (2013) *Critical perspectives on child sexual exploitation and related trafficking*, Basingstoke: Palgrave Macmillan, pp 96–109.

United Nations (1989) The United Nations Convention on the Rights of the Child, UN Office of the High Commissioner for Human Rights.

Warrington, C. (2013) 'Partners in care? Sexually exploited young people's inclusion and exclusion from decision making in safeguarding' in M. Melrose and J. Pearce (eds) *Critical perspectives on child sexual exploitation and related trafficking*, Basingstoke: Palgrave Macmillan, pp 110–25.

Wood, M., Barter, C. and Berridge, D. (2011) *'Standing on my own two feet': disadvantaged teenagers, intimate partner violence and coercive control*, London: NSPCC.

8

Missing children post-Munro

Charlie Hedges

Background

Historically, the importance of missing persons has not been sufficiently recognised, with cases often referred to as 'just another misper' (a common abbreviation for missing person). Children going missing have not always attracted much attention, particularly those who are looked after and/or go missing frequently. Looking back over my past 16 years of involvement in this area, there was real difficulty getting any interest in the subject in the earlier period. However, since the government response to the Munro review (HM Government, 2012), there has been increased momentum in prioritising the risks facing this group of children. This chapter explores the progress made in identifying responses to children going missing and highlights the key challenges that remain in relation to information sharing, integrated working and understanding the full extent of the problem. It also examines the links between children missing and wider exploitation, including sexual exploitation and trafficking, particularly for children in residential care.

There have, of course, been historic peaks of interest, mainly prompted by high-profile cases such as Holly Wells and Jessica Chapman, and Sarah Payne. However, while attention was heightened by these cases, it was not sustained for long and 'missing' once again dipped out of consciousness. A relatively small number of people strive to maintain awareness of the issues.

Madeleine McCann's tragic disappearance in 2007 seemed to be a watershed and the level of interest has been maintained since then. Since that time, a number of other factors have contributed to a higher profile for missing children. The year 2011 was significant in this regard, because of the Munro review and also because of the following milestones:

- 25 May 2011: the government announced the decision to give the responsibility for missing children to the Child Exploitation and Online Protection Centre (CEOP), now a command of the National Crime Agency.
- October 2011: the Office of the Children's Commissioner (OCC) commenced its inquiry into child sexual exploitation (CSE) in groups and gangs, which would identify the links between going missing and this type of abuse (OCC, 2011).
- December 2011: the government published its report, *Missing children and adults: a cross-government strategy* (HM Government, 2011).

These events were followed in June 2012 by a report from the joint inquiry into children who go missing from care (HM Government, 2012), while there continue to be regular meetings of the all-party parliamentary group (APPG) for runaway and missing children.

All of this marked a significant change from the preceding years and interest is being driven forward by actions resulting from these events. I will look at these in more detail to consider what impact they have had and are having on child protection where it relates to missing children. I will also consider whether the legacy of the Munro review has assisted the focus on hearing from children themselves who are at risk of going missing.

The national focus

CEOP has always had a child-centred approach to its work, albeit its main focus has been online abuse. The government decision changed its remit to include offline safety, particularly in relation to missing and abducted children and CSE. The Minister for Crime and Security, James Brokenshire, in his 25 May 2012 announcement, stated:

CEOP's new responsibility for national missing children's services means they can bring their significant child protection expertise to tackle this important issue.

The new team will lead the national response, working in partnership with police forces, non-governmental organisations (NGOs) and the wider child protection community. They will also provide preventative support through the provision of educational tools, products and training to children and professionals, as well as direct operational support to local forces.

Child protection expertise lies at the heart of what CEOP does, with child protection advisers working alongside law enforcement and other experts. The centre also provides expertise to the National Crime Agency, founded in October 2013, because of its duty to safeguard and promote the welfare of children under section 11 of the Children Act 2004.

When supporting police forces in the investigation of difficult and complex cases, it is now the norm for the investigative adviser to be accompanied by a child protection adviser. This means that a strategy for managing the return of a young person can be developed in anticipation of this happening.

Partnership has always been a key element of CEOP's work and is carried through in relation to missing children. Its partnerships with the UK Missing Persons Bureau and Missing People ensure that key national services in relation to missing persons are joined up and avoid duplication of effort.

National partnership agencies

CEOP leads on all matters relating to child abuse and child protection and is the lead agency for missing and abducted children, acting in an advisory role to law enforcement and other agencies. It offers education and professional development and manages Child Rescue Alert and the Missingkids website (http://missingkids.co.uk).

The UK Missing Persons Bureau is the lead agency for missing adults, acting in an advisory role to law enforcement and other agencies. It holds the national database of missing persons and the national database of unidentified persons, bodies and body parts. It is also the custodian of the missing persons DNA database.

Missing People manages the 116000 European standard hotline for missing people, offers support to those who are missing and their families, and produces publicity and appeals for missing persons.

Education and training

CEOP has a long-established educational programme, ThinkuKnow, using ambassadors throughout the UK to deliver child safety messages, which no longer focus solely on online safety. A DVD, *My choice*, was produced in 2011, showing children and parents that there are choices other than running away and how to seek support should running away be the option they are forced to choose (CEOP, 2011).

The Munro reforms emphasised to law enforcement agencies the importance of integrated working with child protection services and, most importantly, that the driver for change would be on practice at local level. Work commenced in 2013 in conjunction with the College of Policing to bring all police training up to date with wider child protection legislation. This is fundamental to influencing practice.

However, while there is recognition nationally of the problem of children missing, there remain significant difficulties in identifying the exact numbers of children missing, compounded by different views on the definition of 'missing' and exacerbated by lack of integrated approaches at the front line. This is being tackled.

Understanding the scale of the problem – the national perspective

The OCC inquiry into CSE in gangs and groups over two years required all relevant agencies to provide evidence of listening to the voices of young people (OCC, 2012b, 2013). Again, building on the focus of the Munro review – hearing directly from children and targeting those most vulnerable – the inquiry has helped maintain momentum in addressing children going missing (Department for Education, 2011).

That missing is integral to exploitation has always been clear to some practitioners but it was only with the publication of the OCC's interim report (OCC, 2012b) that the link was made explicit. The report shows just how significant the incidence of going missing is to sexual exploitation and that it should be treated as an indicator of such activity. The voices of the children who have been the victims of such abuse are extremely powerful and allow everyone to comprehend the tragedies that are being played out across the UK.

Missing children and adults: a cross-government strategy

This strategy built on the government report *The Missing Persons Taskforce: a report with recommendations for improving the multi-agency response to missing incidents* (HM Government, 2010). It was developed in consultation with relevant experts in the field of missing persons and has been the driver for a number of areas of work to improve the way that missing persons of all ages have been dealt with. The strategy resulted in a considerable focus on missing children. Three objectives were set around prevention, protection and provision. This is the first time that a UK government has set a comprehensive strategy on missing persons agreed by all parties as a cross-government strategy.

Joint inquiry into children who go missing from care

Government interest in missing children has continued post-Munro. This inquiry was led across government by the APPG for runaway and missing children and adults and the APPG for looked-after children and care-leavers. It called for evidence from a wide range of sources and published a report that set out a number of recommendations (HM Government, 2012). Four of these were taken forward by the Department for Education, leading to the setting up of working groups to consider how to improve:

- national and local data collection arrangements;
- arrangements and quality of care and support for children placed out of area by their local authorities;
- the overall quality of children's residential provision; and
- the sharing of information between the Office for Standards in Education (Ofsted) and the police service relating to the location of children's homes, involving a change to the regulation that prevented this in the past.

Challenges remaining in identifying children at risk of going missing?

(a) Data and the scale of the problem

Despite more co-ordination from central government post-Munro, understanding the scale of the problem remains difficult. The Association of Chief Police Officers (ACPO, 2005) definition of 'missing' was very wide, potentially capturing every instance of someone not being where they should be, but was adopted by most of the agencies involved in this area of work.

The UK Missing Persons Bureau holds the most comprehensive collection of data through a code of practice introduced in 2009 requiring all UK police forces to report numbers of missing persons to the bureau (UK Missing Persons Bureau, 2009). This has enabled the publication of reports for the years 2010/11 and 2011/12 (UK Missing Persons Bureau, 2011, 2012). The second set of figures shows the following:

- 313,000 people were reported missing to the police, down by 14,000 on the previous year.
- Some people go missing on more than one occasion; this represents 192,000 individuals, down by 216,000 on 2010/11.
- Children and young persons make up 64%; the figure was 66% in the previous report.
- Those reported missing most frequently are 15- to 17-year-olds.

The Children's Society conducts regular research on missing children (The Children's Society, 2011). The charity estimates that the numbers of children reported to the police as missing represent only 68% of the total number. The children who fall into this category are mainly those whose families do not report them missing, either because they do not trust the police or they do not consider them to be missing.

It is interesting to compare UK data with those in other European countries (European Union, 2013). The UK reported 91,230 children missing in 2011; the two next countries in terms of numbers were France, with 52,742, and Germany, with 39,708. While the UK figures are lower than those given by the UK Missing Persons Bureau (possibly owing to the voluntary nature of the request), the comparisons between the countries are significant. No research has been carried out to ascertain why such differences exist but they demonstrate huge uncertainty about the scale of the problem.

There has also been a disparity between the annual figures reported by the Department for Education and the police in relation to missing children, with the gap being so wide as to cause significant concern about our understanding of the numbers. The main reason for the disparity relates to the classification codes for reporting data. While the police count every single incident of missing personS reported to them, local authorities report the numbers of looked-after children who are missing for more than 24 hours.

While data recording has improved, it still does not give a comprehensive picture of all aspects of children who go missing. For this reason, despite the positive steps of the past three years, understanding the scale of the problem provides real challenge to reducing the risks of children going missing and information sharing between areas and services is often poor.

(b) Reducing bureaucracy

For several years, there has also been a drive by the government to reduce bureaucracy in policing, with the investigation of missing persons being one of its priorities. The challenge was to make the process simpler but without creating short cuts that would increase or introduce risks to missing persons. Some work was undertaken by Sussex Police to manage missing person investigations more effectively and to develop a more discerning response involving all agencies (Sussex Police, 2012).

The resultant processes seemed to work, allowing filters to be put in place and ensuring that investigations receive a proportionate rather than a one-size-fits-all response. Coincidentally, this has resulted in a reduction in bureaucracy through less form-filling and a lower number of missing person incidents being reported. It was decided that this model should be piloted in other police forces to consider whether it could be applied elsewhere.

The process introduced a category of 'absent', which caused some concern in various quarters as it was felt that not categorising cases as missing would reduce the attention that they were given.

As discussed earlier under 'Data and the scale of the problem', the numbers of children who are reported missing are significant and picking out those at greatest risk of harm can be difficult. Frequent short-term absences are a typical pattern that occurs. Clearly, there will be risk associated with this type of behaviour, but is the best way to respond by filling out a missing person form? It is clear that responses have become formulaic and do not have true investigative input. It is important that frequent absences are recognised for the risks they pose and responded to in a way that deals with those risks effectively.

(c) Changes to definition and process

The new definition, piloted in Sussex and subsequently adopted by ACPO (2010), is as follows:

- Missing: anyone whose whereabouts cannot be established and where the circumstances are out of character or the context suggests the person may be subject of crime or at risk of harm to themselves or another
- Absent: a person not at a place where they are expected or required to be.

Adding an element of risk to the definition allows judgements to be made about how to deal with the risk, enabling a discerning response to the report. Each case should be treated as an investigation, working in partnership with all relevant agencies to locate the child as quickly as possible.

The category of absent must not be a place to record something then forget about it. When a report is made to the police, the circumstances should be discussed with the person reporting and agreement reached about the correct course of action. If it is to be recorded as absent, review times and interim actions should be agreed and contact maintained to allow ongoing oversight of the case, with escalation to missing or closure considered. Once the child returns, there should be oversight by missing person co-ordinators or those performing a similar role in police stations to identify trends and patterns that may emerge and require further action.

The main intention of the new process is to make it child-centred, responding to incidents in the correct manner, with all agencies working to safeguard the child.

(d) Managing the risk

Another key challenge to addressing children going missing is understanding risk, and owing to the nature of missing person incidents, it is very difficult to develop an accurate risk assessment model. The *Guidance on the management, investigation and recording of missing persons* (ACPO, 2010), adopted by some other agencies, is a collation of questions that should assist in determining what the risk might be in any particular circumstance.

Since Munro, there has been a better understanding of the continuum of risk that sits behind going missing. The risk does not cease simply because missing children return home or to care. Improving understanding of this is still needed but efforts are being made to ensure that this knowledge is delivered to practitioners.

Labels such as 'streetwise' have been incorrectly applied and young people who persistently run away are often considered to be a nuisance or a waste of time. Recognition that risk does not diminish because someone is a regular runaway is more widespread.

(e) Management of the return

The management of risk has also been improved by the expectation of local areas that there will be a robust return interview. This is a two-stage process, with the first part being a 'safe and well' check, usually by the police. The purpose of this is to check the child's welfare and to enquire what has occurred during their disappearance. Often these encounters are not very productive as there is little opportunity to build any form of rapport that would enable the child to disclose anything. One example of good practice has been developed by Staffordshire Police. Here, training takes place for the police and the staff at children's homes to enable the staff to make an assessment of the child and, where appropriate, to record information or seize articles that may be evidence of criminality. More efforts are being made to raise awareness of the importance of these encounters with police officers, with the reminder that their observations of the young person can be a critical part of the investigation, revealing information pertinent to their return even if they will not speak to the officer.

The return interview is the second stage and should take place a while after the return. It is a more structured encounter, designed to build trust and enable the missing child to share his or her experiences with the interviewer, who should be someone who the child is able to trust. These interviews are often conducted by third-party providers skilled at engaging with these individuals. Application of return interviews is varied; while some areas have adopted them, others have discontinued provision (The Children's Society, 2013).

(f) Multi-agency responses

Many reports indicate that no one agency can solve the problems of children who go missing. While it is clear that efforts put into dealing effectively with missing children will improve safeguarding, reduce the number of incidents of going missing and thereby save costs, there remain difficulties in agencies working together.

That said, the development of multi-agency safeguarding hubs (MASHs) has increased significantly (Home Office, 2013). Not all areas adopt the model but some have their own variant where agencies are co-located or work together in other ways. The MASH is intended as a place where all relevant agencies can work together in one place to tackle safeguarding issues. This will usually overcome any concerns about information sharing and having common strategies.

In Gwent, the MASH is being developed around the management of missing children. Early indications are that there are reductions in numbers of children being reported missing and better outcomes for those who do.

As part of the process, all agencies in the Gwent MASH assess the risk to a child on the first occasion that they go missing, based on their history and the missing event. This enables a better understanding of the risk associated with any future episodes of going missing and will be a more rounded assessment than one simply based on the circumstances of disappearance.

Information sharing

Lack of information sharing has been raised in numerous inquiries and is cited as one of the reasons for agencies failing to identify risky situations, thereby not safeguarding children and sometimes resulting in their maltreatment and death. Has this changed since the Munro review? The issue has gained greater prominence and is recognised as something that must be addressed. But it does not always happen. Hearing individuals from different agencies saying there are reasons not to share information still arises. It must be recognised that where child safeguarding is concerned, there must be good reasons for not sharing information with other agencies.

Improvements in information sharing are being made and have been referenced earlier in this chapter.

Trafficked children who go missing

This is a difficult issue to deal with and there are few national data to indicate what the true extent of the scale of the problem really is. Moreover, some local areas, even when identifying children who have gone missing and are likely to be trafficked, are unable to prevent this occurring. In one local authority area, Kent, 18 such children went missing in 2012/13 and were considered to have been trafficked (Kent Safeguarding Children Board, 2013). There are some areas of good practice, mainly based at airports. Both London Gatwick and London Heathrow airports are known for the volume of trafficked children who arrive there en route to other parts of the UK or other countries and both have specific but different responses to respond to the problem that have been in place for a number of years.

Children who have been trafficked come to notice at ports, emerge from the backs of lorries and are found through police raids on cannabis farms, brothels and so forth. Such children have a high propensity for going missing, often due to the pressures put on them by the traffickers. Going missing in these circumstances can be managed and the incidence of disappearing reduced to very small numbers, provided an effective response is in place. Unfortunately, such a response is not universal.

There is still evidence of trafficked children being dealt with in the criminal justice system and sometimes imprisoned rather than being dealt with as victims. More work is needed to raise awareness of the correct assessment of the status of individuals discovered in such situations (OCC, 2012a; Home Office, 2013).

Links between going missing and child sexual exploitation

This is now registered in the awareness of the public, police and other agencies. It is not a new phenomenon but the scale at which it exists has not previously been recognised. Police operations and the subsequent high-profile trials have shocked many people and raised awareness. The links to going missing have been made and the shortcomings of statutory agencies to respond to the risks made public (HMIC, 2013; Rochdale Borough Safeguarding Children Board, 2013).

Operation Retriever in Derbyshire was the first high-profile case that went to court, resulting in nine men being convicted for their part in the abuse of 27 known victims. This was followed by cases in Rochdale, Oxford and Telford, all gaining significant notoriety during 2013, with many investigations and trials held elsewhere. Some of the evidence given during these investigations demonstrated significant levels of running away, with testimony indicating that little notice seemed to be taken of these incidents.

Further research has been conducted in relation to these links (Smeaton, 2013), based on interviews with children, and gives their stories as evidence of the dreadful nature of these situations. It also makes the links between CSE and running away very clear and there are a number of recommendations for improved practices. The ACPO (2012) *Child sexual exploitation action plan* places increasing requirements on local police forces to work with partners to provide problem profiles of CSE at a local level.

Links between children in care and going missing

Generally, it is accepted that looked-after children have a greater propensity for going missing on multiple occasions than those who live at home. This would seem natural: their circumstances are such that they need to be looked after, they have significant issues in their lives and running away is one of the responses to those issues. Two factors have changed in recent years: the increase in private care as a result of the reduction in local authority provision and a shift towards a greater use of foster carers.

The quality of care has been challenged by the APPG on looked-after children who run away and go missing, with evidence presented showing that looked-after children do not get appropriate levels of care (HM Government, 2012).

Out-of-area placements is another issue that has raised concerns, with evidence given to the inquiry that a large proportion of children are placed out of area. There is evidence to suggest that the children arrive at their placement with little or no information given to the host placement and local authority to enable them to properly assess the risks to the child and their propensity for running away. The situation also makes it difficult for their social worker to stay in regular contact and be aware of the issues relating to the child and their placement.

The Office for Standards in Education

This inspection body examines, among other things, the effectiveness of children's care provision. Ofsted inspections look at care placements to evaluate how well they are run and how well the children are cared for and safeguarded. From late 2013, inspectors will be based locally and will be able to build relationships with care providers and other agencies in their area. Police forces have long argued that if they are provided with the locations of children's homes, they can build relationships with staff at the homes and hone their responses to provide an appropriate response to incidents. Until now, this has been hindered by regulations that prevented the sharing of such information. On 1 April 2013, these regulations were changed to allow the routine sharing of addresses with the police, local authorities and the OCC (HM Government, 2013).

The sharing of information between the police and Ofsted to inform the inspection process should enable more accurate inspections to take place.

Attitudes and awareness to missing – going forward

In considering current policy in this country to children missing, there does seem to be improvement since the Munro review, with greater recognition of the best interests of the child, better understanding that child prostitution is not an appropriate term for sexually exploited children and that more consideration needs to be given to the needs of the child rather than those needs the state wishes to impose on them. It is still common, however, to hear practitioners speak about children who regularly go missing as being a nuisance and wasting time, and a lack of understanding of the effects of grooming on a child's behaviour.

Overall, there is a move towards better provision for missing and runaway children, but there is still some way to go to achieve the best standards and to translate national policy into improved outcomes for those most at risk at local level.

References

ACPO (Association of Chief Police Officers) (2005) *Guidance on the management, investigation and recording of missing persons*, London: ACPO.

ACPO (2010) *Guidance on the management, investigation and recording of missing persons*, London: ACPO.

ACPO (2012) *Child sexual exploitation action plan*, London: ACPO.

CEOP (Child Exploitation and Online Protection) Centre (2011) *My choice*, DVD, London: CEOP.

Department for Education (2011) *A child-centred system: the government's response to the Munro review of child protection*, London: The Stationery Office.

European Union (2013) *Missing children in the European Union*, Brussels: EU.

HM Government (2010) *The Missing Persons Taskforce: a report with recommendations for improving the multi-agency response to missing incidents*, London: Home Office.

HM Government (2011) *Missing children and adults: a cross-government strategy*, London: Home Office.

HM Government (2012) *Report from the joint inquiry into children who go missing from care*, London: The Stationery Office.

HM Government (2013) *Joint protocol subject: Her Majesty's Chief Inspector for Education, Children's Services and Skills (HMCI) disclosing details on their register of children's homes with local authorities, the police, the Office of the Children's Commissioner and the Secretary of State for Education*, London: Department for Education.

HMIC (Her Majesty Inspectorate of Constabulary) (2013) *South Yorkshire Police's response to child sexual exploitation: findings of an inspection commissioned by the Police and Crime Commissioner*, London: The Stationery Office.

Home Office (2013) *Multi agency working and early information sharing project: early findings*, London: Home Office.

Kent Safeguarding Children Board (2013) *Annual report*, Kent: KSCB

OCC (Office of the Children's Commissioner) (2011) *Inquiry into child sexual exploitation in gangs and groups*, London: OCC.

OCC (2012a) *Landing in Kent*, London: OCC.

OCC (2012b) 'I thought I was the only one. The only one in the world'. Interim report on child sexual exploitation in gangs and groups, London: OCC.

OCC (2013) 'If only someone had listened'. Final report on child sexual exploitation in gangs and groups, London: OCC.

Rochdale Borough Safeguarding Children Board (2013) Serious Case Report Young Persons 1-7, Rochdale.

Smeaton, E. (2013) Running from hate to what you think is love: the relationship between running away and child sexual exploitation, London: Barnardos.

The Children's Society (2011) Still running, London: The Children's Society.

The Children's Society (2013) Here to listen: return interviews provision for young runaways, London: The Children's Society.

UK Missing Persons Bureau (2009) Code of practice, London: UK Missing Persons Bureau.

UK Missing Persons Bureau (2012). Missing persons data, London: UK Missing Persons Bureau.

UK Missing Persons Bureau (2013) Missing persons: data, London: UK Missing Persons Bureau.

UK Sussex Police (2012) Missing persons policy, Sussex: Sussex Police.

9

Symbolic half-measures? On local safeguarding children boards, their contributions and challenges

Michael Preston-Shoot and Martin Pratt

Introduction

In a speech on child protection, Michael Gove (2012) called for "an open discussion free of cant, obfuscation, emulsifying jargon and euphemism". This chapter, jointly authored by an independent chair of a local safeguarding children board (LSCB) and a director of children's services (DCS), aspires to promote just such open discussion. It offers a reflective critique of the expectations invested in current systems for embedding accountability, assurance and improvements in children's safeguarding in England and Wales, underpinned by evidence drawn from experience and research. Subsequently, Gove (2013) has questioned whether politicians have been "sufficiently systematic, radical and determined" when reforming children's social care, and whether their responses to child protection failures have promoted "a defensive response based on compliance with bureaucratic demands rather than pursuit of excellence". The critique offered in this chapter highlights missed opportunities and simplistic assumptions relating to how LSCBs might best ensure effective and accountable child protection practice.

A chapter in an earlier book (Preston-Shoot, 2012) questioned the hope placed in LSCBs to make a difference in promoting accountability, monitoring effectiveness and generating learning from practice. That chapter concluded that despite examples of innovative practice and leadership investment in creating structures, audit and training programmes, and protocols for information sharing

---

and serious case reviews (SCRs), LSCBs had yet to demonstrate the impact of their work, manage effectively the breadth of their safeguarding responsibilities and engage meaningfully with children and young people.

Updated statutory guidance (HM Government, 2013) restates the importance of LSCBs in providing the effective co-ordination of, and challenge to, safeguarding children services. It increased the responsibilities placed on LSCBs, particularly the function to promote learning and improvement, and modified the accountability architecture, giving greater prominence to the role of local authority chief executive officer (CEO) in appointing and holding to account the independent chair. However, little has been done to remedy the arguable weaknesses in how the LSCB mandate has been configured, namely, the resources available to guarantee board capacity to fulfil its statutory functions, the complexity of legal rules surrounding information sharing, the reliance on permissive rather than directive authority to ensure interagency collaboration, and the assumed independent voice when the majority of board members are on the inside of the safeguarding systems and services being scrutinised. This chapter's title intentionally questions whether the establishment of LSCBs represents a symbolic aspiration rather than a systemically informed intention to devise effective systems for addressing the complexities in safeguarding governance. Such a focus has wider resonance, too, as parliament debates the Care Bill, within which sit proposals to place local safeguarding adults boards on a statutory footing, raising questions as to whether the final shape of the emergent legal rules will perpetuate or avoid systemic weaknesses in governance arrangements experienced by LSCBs.

Little has been written specifically about the operation of LSCBs since that earlier chapter (Preston-Shoot, 2012), although Munro and France (2012), drawing on their earlier case study research of six boards (France et al, 2010), have also explored the challenges faced and questioned the degree to which boards have been able to establish solid foundations. This chapter will develop an analysis of LSCBs, theorising practice and exploring the complexities of the interface between boards and local authorities and the journey towards outstanding performance in safeguarding.

Systems

To be effective, any transformational change in a system requires all the subsystems that constitute effective and accountable children's safeguarding to reinforce rather than frustrate the change effort. Arguably, insufficient attention has been paid by policymakers to this basic principle of systemic change when seeking to create the conditions for LSCB effectiveness.

Legal and resources subsystems

The Children Act 2004 empowers LSCBs to raise resources from partner agencies in order to implement their functions. However, boards cannot require partner agencies to provide resources in cash or kind, a tension aggravated by the impact of financial austerity and the increasing responsibilities given to LSCBs. Capacity is therefore a key issue.

Reviews in Wales (Care and Social Services Inspectorate Wales, 2009; ESTYN et al, 2011) found agency disagreement regarding the funding required to run LSCBs, with widespread variation in contributions and in the ability of boards to harness the collective resources, skills and knowledge of partner agencies. Budgets were a source of tension, resources were insecure and heavy reliance was placed on local authorities. The reviews concluded that this situation was unsustainable, but the Social Services and Well-Being (Wales) Bill 2013 appears silent on whether and how to ensure that resources are forthcoming. A Scottish perspective on child protection committees (Skinner and Bell, 2007), which are similar mechanisms to LSCBs, also found funding levels inadequate and resource arrangements problematic, impacting on the progression of important issues.

Office for Standards in Education (Ofsted) inspections (eg Ofsted, 2010, 2012a, 2013a) have observed that some LSCBs have insufficient budgets to support their work and the professional leadership they can provide, resulting in delays in publishing annual reports and SCRs, conducting multi-agency audit programmes and evaluating the impact of training. Others have emphasised the leadership given by independent chairs (eg Ofsted, 2012b, 2012c) but not commented on funding arrangements to ensure they have the time and support to link effectively into local authority and other organisations' networks and structures, which is a key part of the role (Munro and France, 2012). Indeed, inspection reports remain silent on the impact of how the legal rules regarding budgets have been configured. Neither do they consistently report on how local authority budgets, and the resources available to partner agencies, impact on safeguarding systems. Yet, they are sometimes critical of how important issues, such as child sexual exploitation, have been progressed (eg Ofsted, 2012c). The Ofsted review of the effectiveness of LSCBs, just commencing at the time of writing in late 2013, does however propose a judgement on whether partners are making a proportionate financial and resource contribution to the work of the board. It remains to be seen whether this in itself will be a sufficient corrective.

Similarly, the legal rules, as currently configured, do not enable LSCBs to compel agencies to participate, for example in audits. Once again, inspections have sharply criticised boards for shortcomings in partnership working and the limited engagement of some statutory partners in performance review and practice development (eg Ofsted, 2013b). However, the silence in the legal rules regarding powers to engage the disengaged remains unacknowledged, with the consequence that LSCBs 'lack teeth' (Horwath, 2010) and remain reliant on agencies taking seriously their decisions and business plans (Munro and France, 2012).

Information-sharing legislation (Data Protection Act 1998) may also frustrate key board functions. It is easy to state that LSCBs require information to monitor whether services are making a difference and to inform the development of prevention and protection interventions in response to such issues as child sexual exploitation, poverty and neglect (Munro, 2012). However, where audit focuses solely on reviewing individual cases in order to embed learning in practice, information sharing between partner agencies may prove less problematic than where similar cases are collated to explore the safety and effectiveness of safeguarding policies, systems and practices. The Children, Schools and Families Act 2010 conferred a power on LSCBs to require the provision of information to assist with the performance of their functions. However, the Health and Social Care

Act 2012 failed to consider information sharing within and beyond organisations in the new National Health Service (NHS) architecture in England for safeguarding, where the focus is service improvement rather than benefit to a particular child. Currently, therefore, Data Protection Act 1998 constraints may limit how LSCBs can audit policy and practice effectiveness across types of cases. Meanwhile, Ofsted (eg 2012c) criticises boards for ineffective and inadequate information sharing.

LSCBs themselves are coming under increasing legal scrutiny, which underlines the importance of members having knowledge of relevant legal rules and access to lawyers. Examples revolving around SCRs illustrate the importance of abiding by the requirements of administrative law when reaching decisions, of balancing human rights with data protection and accountability considerations, and of following statutory guidance. The Equality and Human Rights Commission (EHRC, 2012) has suggested that SCRs might not meet a public body's obligations to uphold the right to life if they do not establish the cause of death and involve the family, and if they are not independent of the agencies involved and carried out in public. There may be Human Rights Act 1998 implications if LSCBs fail to intervene in cases of serious safeguarding failings by partner agencies, such as in the juvenile secure estate.

Care must be taken when deciding whether to commission an SCR, challenging the responses from organisations involved and determining its scope (*R. Webster v Swindon Local Safeguarding Children Board*, 2009). Contributors to the individual management reviews that ultimately inform the overview report should know that these reports may have to be disclosed to coroners. This may affect the candour required from those whose work and decisions are scrutinised to ensure open and critical evaluation of individual and agency practice (*Worcestershire County Council and Another v HM Coroner for the County of Worcestershire*, 2013).

Public interest in full disclosure of reviews will continue to be tested, notwithstanding risks to surviving family members (*Torney v Information Commissioner and the Regional Health and Social Care Board*, 2013). That publication of SCRs must conform to Data Protection Act 1998 requirements for the management and disclosure of information (HM Government, 2013) may not be the final word. The interface between different systems for ensuring accountability and lesson learning is not necessarily seamless.

Moreover, the introduction of panels of independent experts to help LSCBs make the right decisions about conducting and publishing SCRs (HM Government, 2013) indicates that for boards, and particularly for their independent chairs, the courts will not be the only body to scrutinise their decision-making in this most sensitive area of their work.

Governance and accountability subsystems

Some LSCBs have been criticised for governance failures, such as unrealistic and ineffective business and work plans (Ofsted, 2012b). Partnership working, specifically engagement by some statutory partners, has remained a challenge (Ofsted, 2013a, 2013b, 2013c). Elected member understanding and participation has proved variable (HM Government, 2008; Care and Social Services Inspectorate Wales, 2009), although the interface with scrutiny committees can work effectively (Ofsted, 2013b). Thus, the work of some boards may be underdeveloped. However, the legal rules for cohesive multi-agency working are similarly underdeveloped because LSCBs can neither command agencies to participate nor impose sanctions if they fail to comply with their statutory obligations. Experience has also demonstrated that members may not consistently be able to set aside organisational allegiances and affiliations in favour of board responsibilities (Munro and France, 2012) because of their settings' constraints and imperatives. The independent voice and the externality of challenge may come to rest on the (stretched) resourcing (time, support, knowledge and skills) of the independent chair and lay members.

The unique role of the lead member for children's services (LMCS), as the only member of the LSCB with a mandate for the local political leadership of children's services and the only one given the somewhat ambiguous role of 'participating observer', is rarely commented on. For example, the grade descriptors contained in Ofsted's (2013e) review of effectiveness of LSCBs is silent on this aspect of the board's work or governance. *Working together* (HM Government, 2013) makes it clear that the LMCS should regularly attend meetings and receive the papers but says nothing about the participatory aspect of the role. While the engagement of the LMCS is absolutely critical to the effective leadership of safeguarding work at a local level, it is difficult to discern the impact of their inclusion in the LSCB in this way. The decision, taken in the febrile atmosphere following the publication of the Peter Connelly SCR, to create a role that has either apparently unfulfilled potential or is a rather awkward political 'fix' in response to understandable concerns about political ownership and oversight of child protection at the time has yet to be vindicated.

Arguably, the way the role of the LMCS was incorporated into the work of the LSCB contrasts markedly with the role accorded to the same position when health and wellbeing boards (HWBs) were established. In this instance, statutory members of the HWB, a combination of members, officers and other senior partners, share similar roles, powers and responsibilities. Participating observer status is not used as a way of maintaining a distinction between elected representatives and others.

LSCBs comprise one piece in an increasingly complex governance and accountability jigsaw. The pieces may not fit neatly and the emergent picture may not be seen by all participants of different committees and boards, or indeed ultimately be drawn together in one place. What has been created hardly mirrors the clear and sharp accountability that Gove (2013) has prioritised. Criticism has been voiced of the complex partnership and organisational arrangements, which may mean that people sit at the same tables, responsibilities are blurred, management of cross-cutting issues is unclear and ownership of specific issues, such as domestic violence or hate crime, is muddled (ESTYN et al, 2011; Ofsted, 2012a). The simplistic response is to recommend that LSCBs must work effectively with other boards, such as HWBs, to ensure coherence and connectivity between key strategic plans, information sharing and two-way holding to account (Ofsted, 2012b, 2012c, 2013d). It is significant that in its response to the consultation on the Ofsted review of effectiveness of LSCB proposals, the Association of Directors of Children's Services (2013a) stated that its primary concern was that the work of the LSCB should be understood in the local partnership context where the range of boards, trusts and other partnership forums is complex and increasingly diverse.

A more systemic approach would question why LSCBs and local safeguarding adult boards are not statutory members of HWBs and whether simplification and clarification of partnership arrangements are urgently necessary (ESTYN et al, 2011) in order to ensure a clear overview of significant issues and the effectiveness of work in safeguarding children and adults at risk. The authors, however, recognise and support the expectation set out in *Working together* (HM Government, 2013): 'In order to provide effective scrutiny, the LSCB should be independent. It should not be subordinate to, nor subsumed within, other local structures.' So, the proposition that independent chairs might become statutory members of HWBs should not be taken to imply a subsumed or subordinate role for the LSCB.

Review subsystem

The Children, Schools and Families Act 2010 permitted the Secretary of State to make regulations to provide for the review of the performance of LSCBs. Now implemented, following recommendations that LSCBs should be scrutinised by an inspectorate (ESTYN et al, 2011; Munro, 2012) and concerns about weak leadership (Ofsted, 2010, 2012a, 2012b), this has allowed Ofsted (2013e) to consult on the review framework itself. Judgments about effectiveness will be based on compliance with statutory guidance, evidence of co-ordination of the work of statutory partners and monitoring effectiveness, and evaluation for impact of multi-agency training on management and practice. Policies and procedures must be in place and understood, with practice challenge and audits driving improvements. SCRs, audits and reviews should promote learning with children and practitioners. Monitoring of front-line practice and the quality of management oversight should be evident, with co-ordinated activity between the HWB, LSCB and other strategic partnerships and evidence that this leads to improvement priorities. LSCBs should be active in informing and planning services via assessments of multiagency practice, with the annual report providing a rigorous and transparent assessment of the performance and effectiveness of local services. The DCS should work closely with the board's independent chair, with the local authority CEO actively holding the latter accountable for the LSCB's effectiveness.

Systemically, there are several issues with these review proposals. First, Ofsted (2013e) will judge LSCB effectiveness against all safeguarding activity, including early help, core child protection activities and local priorities. This contradicts research evidence, which has demonstrated that LSCBs are more effective when focusing realistically on a small number of strategic priorities (Care and Social Services Inspectorate Wales, 2009; Munro and France, 2012). Second, workforce changes in partner agencies impact on multi-agency working, sometimes detrimentally for LSCBs (Ofsted, 2010) and sometimes beneficially (Ofsted, 2012a, 2012b), over which they may have little influence or control. Increasingly, boards are being positioned to drive improvement across local child protection systems (eg Ofsted, 2013a), drawing on dynamic qualitative performance analysis that identifies strengths, weaknesses and priorities. However, leadership within the local authority may well have demanding change agendas on which to focus, which will impact on the outcomes of the board's work, or, alternatively, boards may have been looking for leadership contributions from senior managers on whose watch child protection systems have shown variable or poor decision-making, sharing of information, quality of assessments and management of risk (see Ofsted, 2010, 2012b, 2012c). Third, limited notice will be given of a forthcoming review, meaning that LSCBs may well maintain a state of inspection-readiness, against which Munro (2011) in her inquiry advised.

Fourth, the expectation that LSCBs will effectively evaluate performance data to inform service planning and delivery ignores the reality that they cannot command agencies to co-operate. Effectively, challenge relies on openness and consent. Equally, LSCBs have no power to impose strategic direction or operational practices on partner agencies (ESTYN et al, 2011; Skinner and Bell, 2007), which may reduce the impact outcome of any analysis, challenge and advice offered by LSCBs from performance data evaluation and learning and improvement discussions. Fifth, Ofsted proposes to evaluate how effectively LSCBs monitor and assess the quality and effectiveness of local authorities and their partners. This again presupposes openness and transparency from the partners and constructive relationships between agencies, for example between commissioners and providers in the NHS. However, experience and inquiries have found that boards may not be told of serious shortcomings in organisational practices and may be blocked when seeking to be well informed about local safeguarding issues (ESTYN and Care and Social Services Inspectorate Wales, 2011). An LSCB knows what questions to ask and what data to expect but its performance may be frustrated by the unwillingness of partners to engage transparently and by the limited availability of high-quality information with which to monitor and challenge practice effectively (Ofsted, 2013b).

Sixth, LSCBs cannot demand sufficient resources for audits and the analysis of qualitative data with which to interrogate quantitative performance indicators. Considerable staff time is required to engage in learning and improvement across a wide span of safeguarding, from early help, through risk management and direct work with children and families, to quality supervision and recording and the engagement of communities in children's safeguarding. A board's ability to improve practice relies on the willingness of agencies to invest in it. Put another way, the reality of children's safeguarding, and the LSCB position within it, is altogether more complex than the review proposals acknowledge. Boards do not operate in isolation from their context (Munro and France, 2012). Indeed, Ofsted itself has judged that LSCBs may function very well but be unable to impact on practice quality (eg Ofsted, 2012d). Moreover, an interesting judgement, passed without comment in several Ofsted inspections (2013a, 2013b), has been that undue emphasis has been given to data that relate to compliance with targets, such as child protection assessment timeframes, rather than the actual quality of service delivery. Yet, what has been privileged in centrally imposed definitions of excellence will inevitably be what local safeguarding agencies foreground (Ayre and Preston-Shoot, 2010).

Purposes and effectiveness in the existing context

LSCBs have a diverse, ambitious and complex remit (Munro and France, 2012), but to what degree is its accomplishment feasible? Concerns have been expressed that boards have not been effective in complying with statutory guidance and in fulfilling their responsibilities (ESTYN et al, 2011; Ofsted, 2012c), some reasons for which have already been explored. Nonetheless, some LSCBs have been assessed as functioning well (Ofsted, 2012d, 2013f).

Thus, within existing legal, regulatory and administrative constraints, what are the characteristics of effective LSCBs and what are the challenges to be overcome?

Scrutiny

One challenge to be negotiated is that of capacity. Ofsted (2012a, 2012b) has acknowledged that LSCBs may not have the resources to scrutinise practice in depth but has compounded the problem by recommending improvements across the full range of child protection practice (Ofsted, 2012a) and in relation to specific priorities such as child sexual exploitation (Ofsted, 2012c), despite research evidence that found boards more effective when realistic about agendas for change (Munro and France, 2012).

LSCBs may be hampered by not knowing what is happening in practice because they are kept at a distance and frustrated in challenging agencies and in leading practice improvements. Local authorities have not always had a reflective, open and learning culture. Boards may sometimes have failed to take decisive action but equally there have been occasions when management performance reports have failed to highlight the experiences of and risks to children (ESTYN and Care and Social Services Inspectorate Wales, 2011; Ofsted, 2012b). Boards therefore face a challenge of negotiating entry and reaching into the cultures and practices of their member organisations. The challenge of reach then extends to engaging with practitioners and children in order to inform practice evaluation, questioning and development (Skinner and Bell, 2007; ESTYN et al, 2011; Ofsted, 2012c).

LSCBs may be hampered, too, by significant underdevelopment of performance management systems, including audits, tracking of trends, analysis and delivery of agreed action plans (Skinner and Bell, 2007; ESTYN et al, 2011; Ofsted, 2012a, 2012b, 2012c, 2013a, 2013b), as well as by the complexity and range of quantitative and qualitative indicators of what 'good' looks like for children, the team around the child, the organisations around the team and the board around the organisations. Moreover, impact of the board's activity may not result in sustained improvements to services (Ofsted, 2013a, 2013b). This may be due to the size of the transformation challenge facing some local authorities, coupled with necessary subsystem changes being overlooked, being slow in pace or actually undermining the potential for practice improvement: budgets, legal mandate for LSCBs, local authority operational and management capacity, caseload demands and workforce supply, data analysis, and research expertise.

Accountability

Concerns about the ability of LSCBs and elected representatives to hold agencies accountable for practice standards have emerged fairly consistently from the inspections and inquiries drawn on earlier. In addition to the reasons already explored, the challenge of challenging itself may have been underestimated. Research has concluded that professionals are hesitant to challenge the practice and decisions of others (Driscoll, 2009), perhaps uncertain about the trust required, unclear about their responsibilities or cognisant of the very real difficulties under which organisations in the public sector are currently labouring. It is also difficult to step back from systems of which one is a part in order to effectively challenge one's own contribution and that of others. Moreover, the proliferation of settings where LSCB members meet, and the multiple 'hats' they are expected to wear, adds to the complexity of trying to establish effective processes and relationships where effective challenge can take place (Horwath, 2010; Munro and France, 2012).

Leadership

Inquiries and inspections have concluded that effective leadership is crucial but is not always being delivered (ESTYN et al, 2011; Ofsted, 2012a, 2012b, 2012c). However, in a critique reminiscent of challenges to analyses contained in SCRs, their explorations often do not answer the 'Why?' question. Significant contributory factors have been explored earlier. Thus, the capacity of independent chairs and lay members to engage all the safeguarding communities, ensure robust business plans and draw on the engagement of partner agencies will depend on the resources and commitments available.

One further clue emerges from the observation that a change of DCS or independent chair can prove significant in opening up possibilities for service improvement (Ofsted, 2012b, 2012c, 2013d), the corollary being that an LSCB may not be able to lead improvements to practice when senior leadership in partner agencies is ineffective in supporting that change agenda (Ofsted, 2013a). LSCB influence is highly dependent on the quality of leadership provided by its members (Horwath, 2010) and on the degree to which these senior managers have support and operational capacity from middle-level managers in each partner agency. What we do know is that an LSCB, if it is to be an effective and dynamic forum for the exercise of mutual or collective accountability, needs clear and unambiguous leadership. This leadership does not, indeed cannot, reside in one person, but requires a form of systems leadership (Virtual Staff College, 2011) distributed among members of the board, with each accepting that an open culture that values trust and challenge is the only way to ensure the integrity of the system and the security of the individual organisations within it. This does not, of course, guarantee the safety of every child in the LSCB's area, but it does mean that the board has an accurate view of the safeguarding system's vulnerabilities and can therefore act to challenge practice and support rapid improvement. It appears to be the case in examples of effective safeguarding systems that this type of distributive systems leadership, which relies on the complementary but distinct roles of independent chair, DCS and CEO, is exercised in a way that is collaborative but visibly non-collusive.

171

Relationships

Organisations and systems are only as effective as the people and their relationships within them. Good leadership is dependent on leaders' personal qualities, values, competence and behaviours (Horwath, 2010), on technical knowledge and relationship competence (Munro and France, 2012). Good governance requires truth-telling, a willingness to admit mistakes and anxiety, open information sharing, and transparency. It involves being relational and promoting dialogue (Hope-Hailey et al, 2012). With such ingredients, boards are more likely to be effective (Care and Social Services Inspectorate Wales, 2009). However, some LSCBs have been criticised for failing to provide leadership (eg Ofsted, 2013a) and, arguably, in the proliferation of guidance for and mounting expectations on LSCBs, insufficient attention has been paid to relationship issues.

The challenge of challenge

The challenge of challenging peers and colleagues has already been referred to (Driscoll, 2009). Yet, if the partners around the LSCB table are to be effective participants in the mission to safeguard local children, a culture must be led, developed and implemented that promotes openness and values challenge. The board, in its practices, substructures and meetings, has to provide legitimate and positive methods for evidence-based, learning-focused, improvement-oriented challenge. The new requirement to maintain a learning and development framework (HM Government, 2013) provides an ideal opportunity for LSCBs to review and renew, or where necessary establish, both the mechanism for and the culture in which such challenge should be exercised. In essence, it requires boards to lead their local safeguarding systems in a way that promotes dynamic accountability within the system rather than providing a quasi-inspectoral challenge from the outside.

Nonetheless, some LSCBs clearly struggle to develop a culture where challenge can drive service improvement (eg Ofsted, 2012a), perhaps on occasion because members perceive the DCS as unduly controlling (Munro and France, 2012). Members may experience difficulty in challenging a system of which they are a part, and those with greater independence or distance from operational practice, the lay members and independent chair – will gradually also become embedded in the system. Members may bring different orientations to LSCB membership. Some may not wish to disturb what they perceive to be a working equilibrium in multi-agency relationships. Some may seek to overcome particular problems or achieve specific targets. Some may wish to make sense of and transform safeguarding systems. Some may want to explore potential futures and map possibilities. This partly reflects different appetites for change and partly revolves around what members may include within the concept of safeguarding.

Triangular relationships

According to the National Leadership Qualities Framework for Directors and Senior Leaders in Children's Services (Virtual Staff College, 2011), 'The Chief Executive and the Lead Member comprise the most vital peer relationships for DCSs and these can be both challenges to solve and resources to utilise.' It is clear that in the context of safeguarding children, the relationship with the independent chair, although necessarily different, is equally vital. Indeed, since the changed accountability arrangements for independent chairs were introduced (HM Government, 2013), the crucial triangular relationship is that between the independent chair, the DCS and the local authority CEO because it is here that the nexus of scrutiny, direction and accountability resides. As discussed earlier, the role of the LMCS is crucial for the effective political leadership of children's services but is somewhat ambiguous in relation to the functioning of the LSCB. We might refer to this as the 'three plus one' model.

Gove (2012) argued that there was a potential conflict of interest when the DCS was responsible for appointing the independent chair. Subsequently, Gove (2013) has called on CEOs to take their new responsibilities seriously and to fund the work of independent chairs properly. Changing the appointment process does not automatically remove all potential conflicts of interest or, in the context of decimated local authority budgets, ensure appropriate funding. Moreover, triangular relationships have the potential to be equally problematic. For example, organisational and political differences between the DCS and CEO may mean that each may seek a personal relationship with the independent chair to the exclusion of the other. Equally, the CEO and DCS may combine to exclude the independent chair and the board from knowledge of serious safeguarding concerns (eg ESTYN and Care and Social Services Inspectorate Wales, 2011). Either way, the LSCB's effectiveness as a vehicle for promoting learning and driving improvements will be compromised. An additional complexity has been introduced (HM Government, 2013), with the CEO having responsibility for appointing the LSCB chair and holding them accountable for the board's effectiveness while the DCS has statutory responsibility for children's services (Department for Education, 2013). The independent chair must feel able to work with and challenge each without being perceived to have aligned more closely with one rather than the other.

Remoteness

Aside from the relationships between the senior leadership of the local safeguarding system and the relationship between the LSCB members themselves is the crucial systemic relationship between the board and front-line practitioners. If the LSCB is remote, relying on a narrow set of quantitative performance measures and the uncritical self-reporting of agency representatives, it is unable to assess accurately the effectiveness and vulnerabilities of the local system and prone to creating a culture of false assurance. Hearing the authentic voice of practice across the relevant disciplines and communities of practice and understanding the 'lived reality' of practitioners engaged with safeguarding work, from early help through to child protection interventions, is an essential aspect of the LSCB's work. It is only by systematically addressing this relationship that the board can form any meaningful view about how the thresholds for intervention are operating and how responsive the system is to escalating concerns.

Inspections and research have reported on the distance between LSCBs and front-line practice and advised members to feed back to their own staff the priorities identified by LSCBs and the improvements they are seeking (Skinner and Bell, 2007; Care and Social Services Inspectorate Wales, 2009; Ofsted, 2013b). It remains true that, to improve practice, LSCBs must know what is happening in practice (Morrison, 2010), which includes how staff understand organisational messages about priorities, react to workload pressures, audit and scrutiny, and experience their workplaces as potential settings for learning. It includes, too, how children and their families experience standards of practice.

Engagement

A key aspect of this relationship with practitioners, the relationship between the board members and the interpersonal relationship between the system's senior leaders is engagement. This is the mechanism by which effective challenge and mutual accountability is realised. It is through engagement with rather than observation of the local safeguarding system that the individuals responsible for its effective operation become part of an improvement dynamic. Thus, LSCBs are more likely to be effective when there is clear commitment from all partners (Care and Social Services Inspectorate Wales, 2009), successful negotiation of shared values and vision (Skinner and Bell, 2007), and acceptance of the roles, influence, status and authority that different parties bring (Skinner and Bell, 2007; Munro and France, 2012). However, the level of commitment of some agencies remains a concern (HM Government, 2008; Ofsted, 2013b).

For some DCSs, the variability in the quality and experience of independent chairs has been a concern, a key issue being the way in which the 'independent' part of the title has been interpreted. At worst, this is experienced as the chair having free rein to commentate but without acknowledging the distinct but nonetheless dynamic and active role they have in shaping the nature of local practice. The independent chair is and should be independent of the local authority and any of the other partners, so they are able to support, challenge and, where necessary, intervene without fear or favour. They should not, however, act as if they are independent of the safeguarding system, an informed spectator able to offer an independent commentary; they are, in fact, very much a player within it, albeit with a unique and distinctive role. Similarly, it is a common criticism of DCSs that some tend to endure rather than engage the independent chair, trying to control and manage the relationship rather than collaborate in a way that should never be comfortable but is rigorous, mutually challenging and open. Once again, particular dynamics may emerge between the independent chair and DCS, CEO or other board members. 'You are the expert' may see considerable hope and responsibility placed on the independent chair, whose interventions may then be resisted. The 'I am the expert' position may see LSCB members attempt to undermine, sidestep or disqualify the independent chair. The chair may also be reminded of their role, followed by implicit or explicit 'if you dare' or 'don't you dare' communications. Once again, systemic understanding and relational skills will be called for to navigate these complexities, triggered as they may be by understandable anxieties surrounding the child protection task.

Communication and trust

The openness necessary for mutual accountability to function relies on honest communication between the key players; this is particularly true where it relates to systemic risk, adequacy of resources or operational failings. This open communication is an absolute prerequisite if trust between partners is to be established, developed and maintained. Without it, LSCBs are unlikely to be able to evaluate the effectiveness of the help being provided to children and families, assess whether LSCB partners are fulfilling their statutory obligations and quality-assure practice: in short, to fulfil their statutory functions (HM Government, 2013). In reality, there are a number of drivers that potentially inhibit or impede such communication. For example, a combination of media coverage of child maltreatment and murder cases and the impact of an inspection framework that provides single-word summative judgements on the working of complex systems (Association of Directors of Children's Services, 2013b) creates a cultural context that can lead to closed, anxious and distorted communication. Similarly, the extent to which the executive or political leadership of partner agencies mandate their representatives on the LSCB to adopt an open and self-critical stance can lead to asymmetrical degrees of openness, which, in turn, limits trust and promotes similar behaviour in others. Since the personal, professional and organisational stakes are high, open communication, the very thing that promotes trust and therefore has the potential to improve the effectiveness and responsiveness of the safeguarding system, can be undermined.

Two examples illustrate the point. In one inspection (Ofsted, 2013b), the LSCB's effectiveness was hampered by low trust between partners and the poor engagement of some. In another (ESTYN and Care and Social Services Inspectorate Wales, 2011), local authority senior managers minimised safeguarding concerns and did not report openly to the LSCB. This meant the board could not make an effective evaluation of safeguarding practice.

Personnel change

In order to be effective, an LSCB requires a challenging but collegiate culture based around a common understanding of the needs of the local population, a shared analysis of the effectiveness and vulnerabilities of the existing system, engagement with each other and front-line practice, and open communication promoting trust and purposeful activity leading to learning and improvement. However, it also requires courageous leaders willing to model the personal and organisational behaviours required to build resilience into the system and increase the likelihood of assuring effective safeguarding services. This means that changes in key personnel can have a profound impact on the functioning of the board, for good or ill (eg Ofsted, 2012a, 2012c, 2013d). There is therefore a degree of fragility in the model precisely because it is reliant on the quality and the combination of local leadership and on permissive rather than directive authority to ensure interagency collaboration. Moreover, positive leadership contributions may remain reliant on individuals rather than their components becoming embedded in the LSCB and surrounding organisational systems (Care and Social Services Inspectorate Wales, 2009).

Complexity

The complexities outlined earlier mean that simple linear judgements of LSCBs are inappropriate and that linking an evaluative grade for an LSCB with that given to the relevant local authority is questionable. The mandate inherited by LSCBs represents the best and worse, or, more accurately, central government use and distrust, of localism. Distrust emerges through the rhetoric and final decisions regarding publication in full of SCRs and the creation of a panel to oversee commissioning decisions. Use is seen in the creation of LSCBs to challenge child protection systems but then failing to guarantee sufficient resources centrally or legal powers for business effectiveness.

Figure 9.1 captures some of this complexity, but further elaboration is possible if one introduces an 'improving' category for either or both LSCBs and local authorities in all but the top-left quadrant. Thus, an inspection may reveal a well-functioning board in terms of a focused business plan, compliance with statutory requirements and effective chairing, but with limited impact on the quality of strategic management and practice – the bottom-left quadrant (Ofsted, 2012d). Alternatively, a possible scenario is of senior managers who may be driving improvements but with the board yet to play much part in this, either because of the style of the DCS or because of weaknesses within it (top-right quadrant). The top-left quadrant represents a resilient, self-critical, responsive, learning and improving system (Ofsted, 2012e). The bottom-right quadrant represents a situation where neither the board nor senior agency leaders are yet providing the necessary leadership and strategic management of practice (eg Ofsted, 2012a, 2012b).

Figure 9.1 Effectiveness of LSCBs

Strong LSCB and good local authority	Weak LSCB and good local authority
Strong LSCB and inadequate local authority	Weak LSCB and inadequate local authority

Conclusion

Munro and France (2012) have concluded that some of the principles underpinning LSCBs may have contributed to difficulties and that, even if boards are operating effectively, improvement in outcomes for children may be neither visible nor actual. Ofsted inspection reports often criticise LSCBs for lack of evidence of impact. However, as this chapter has argued, to release the potential of LSCBs to be dynamic components of safeguarding systems requires systems change at national policy level as well as locally in organisational, relational and practice systems. To improve the quality and accountability of child protection provision requires more than simply the publication of SCRs. Gove (2012, 2013) was right to point to structural impediments to greater openness and accountability and to question the inconsistent quality of child protection services, but the failure to appreciate the strengths and weaknesses within the LSCB mandate risks them becoming a cherished symbol that no one wishes to question rather than a feature that can really make a difference.

References

Association of Directors of Children's Services (ADCS) (2013a) *Response to Ofsted consultation on the proposed review of the effectiveness of LSCBs*, Manchester: ADCS.

Association of Directors of Children's Services (ADCS) (2013b) Press statement, 25 September, Manchester: ADCS.

Ayre, P. and Preston-Shoot, M. (eds) (2010) *Children's services at the crossroads: a critical evaluation of contemporary policy for practice*, Lyme Regis: Russell House Publishing.

Care and Social Services Inspectorate Wales (2009) *Safeguarding and protecting children in Wales. The review of local authority social services and local safeguarding children boards*, Cardiff: Welsh Assembly Government.

Department for Education (2013) *Statutory guidance on the roles and responsibilities of the director of children's services and the lead member for children's services*, London: The Stationery Office.

Driscoll, J. (2009) 'Prevalence, people and processes: a consideration of the implications of Lord Laming's progress report on the protection of children in England', *Child Abuse Review*, 18, 333–345.

EHRC (Equality and Human Rights Commission) (2012) *How fair is Britain? An assessment of how well public authorities protect human rights*, Manchester: EHRC.

ESTYN (Her Majesty's Inspectorate for Education and Training in Wales) and Care and Social Services Inspectorate Wales (2011) *Joint investigation into the handling and management of allegations of professional abuse and the arrangements for safeguarding and protecting children in education services in Pembrokeshire County Council*, Cardiff: The Stationery Office.

ESTYN, Healthcare Inspectorate Wales, Care and Social Services Inspectorate Wales, HMI Probation and Her Majesty's Inspectorate of Constabulary (2011) *Joint inspection of local safeguarding children boards: overview*, Merthyr Tydfil: CSSIW.

France, A., Munro, E.R. and Waring, A. (2010) *The evaluation of arrangements for effective operation of the new local safeguarding children boards in England – final report*, London: Department for Education.

Gove, M. (2012) 'The failure of child protection and the need for a fresh start', Speech delivered on 16 November.

Gove, M. (2013) 'Getting it right for children in need', Speech delivered on 12 November.

HM Government (2008) *Safeguarding children. The third joint chief inspectors' report on arrangements to safeguard children*, London: The Stationery Office.

HM Government (2013) *Working together to safeguard children. A guide to inter-agency working to safeguard and promote the welfare of children*, London: The Stationery Office.

Hope-Hailey, V., Searle, R. and Dietz, G. (2012) *Where has all the trust gone?*, London: Chartered Institute of Personnel and Development (CIPD).

Horwath, J. (2010) 'Rearing a toothless tiger? From area child protection committee to local safeguarding children board', *Journal of Children's Services*, 5(3), 37–47.

Morrison, T. (2010) 'The strategic leadership of complex practice: opportunities and challenges', *Child Abuse Review*, 19, 312–29.

Munro, E. (2011) *The Munro review of child protection. Final report: a child-centred system*, London: The Stationery Office.

Munro, E. (2012) *The Munro review of child protection. Progress report: moving towards a child-centred system*, London: The Stationery Office.

Munro, E.R. and France, A. (2012) 'Implementing local safeguarding children boards: managing complexity and ambiguity', *Child and Family Social Work*, 17, 337–346.

Ofsted (Office for Standards in Education) (2010) *Inspection of safeguarding and looked after children services: Birmingham*, Manchester: Ofsted.

Ofsted (2012a) *Inspection of local authority arrangements for the protection of children: Rochdale Metropolitan Borough Council*, Manchester: Ofsted.

Ofsted (2012b) *Inspection of local authority arrangements for the protection of children: Doncaster Metropolitan Borough Council*, Manchester: Ofsted.

Ofsted (2012c) *Inspection of local authority arrangements for the protection of children: Birmingham City Council*, Manchester: Ofsted.

Ofsted (2012d) *Inspection of local authority arrangements for the protection of children: Cambridgeshire County Council*, Manchester: Ofsted.

Ofsted (2012e) *Inspection of safeguarding and looked after children services: London Borough of Lambeth*, Manchester: Ofsted.

Ofsted (2013a) *Inspection of local authority arrangements for the protection of children: Northamptonshire County Council*, Manchester: Ofsted.

Ofsted (2013b) *Inspection of local authority arrangements for the protection of children: Norfolk County Council*, Manchester: Ofsted.

Ofsted (2013c) *Inspection of local authority arrangements for the protection of children: Bedford Borough Council*, Manchester: Ofsted.

Ofsted (2013d) *Inspection of local authority arrangements for the protection of children: Peterborough Borough Council*, Manchester: Ofsted.

Ofsted (2013e) *Framework and evaluation schedule for the inspections of services for children in need of help and protection, children looked after and care leavers. Reviews of local safeguarding children boards*, Manchester: Ofsted.

Ofsted (2013f) *Inspection of local authority arrangements for the protection of children: Suffolk County Council*, Manchester: Ofsted.

Preston-Shoot, M. (2012) 'Local safeguarding children boards: faith, hope and evidence', in M. Blyth and E. Solomon (eds) *Effective safeguarding for children and young people: what next after Munro?*, Bristol: Policy Press, pp 25–50.

Skinner, K. and Bell, L. (2007) 'Changing structures: necessary but not sufficient', *Child Abuse Review*, 16, 209–22.

Virtual Staff College (2011) *National leadership qualities framework for directors and senior leaders of children's services*, Nottingham and Manchester:VSC, p 13.

Case law references

R. Webster v Swindon Local Safeguarding Children Board [2009] EWHC 2755 (Admin).

Torney v Information Commissioner and the Regional Health and Social Care Board [2013] UKFTT EA/2012/0143.

Worcestershire County Council and Another v HM Coroner for the County of Worcestershire [2013] EWHC 1711 (QB).

Conclusion

Maggie Blyth

Implementing the Munro reforms

In a precursor to this volume (Blyth and Solomon, 2012), the editors concluded that while there was overall support from government, professionals and academics for Professor Munro's reforms, there was little information on the detail of implementation. Consequently, there remained some ambiguity about how the necessary changes in improved outcomes for the most vulnerable children and young people would occur. Furthermore, concerns were expressed that a narrow definition of child protection work would undermine progress begun a decade ago under the *Every child matters* agenda to make safeguarding 'everybody's business' (Department for Education, 2004). Indeed, many of the Munro recommendations focused on changing social work practice, with less overt attention given to the wider multi-agency framework in which the child protection system sits. This volume reviews the Munro reforms (Munro, 2011) through a multi-agency lens.

The conclusions of the previous volume highlighted a number of overlapping challenges to the implementation of the Munro review, some echoed by Munro herself in her own review of progress (Munro, 2012). These included: the capacity of the workforce; diminishing public sector resources; the future of early intervention approaches and partnership working; the risk of unintended consequences; and the impact of wider public sector reforms affecting the National Health Service (NHS) and schools. This volume has given attention to these areas, which are dealt with in the following text.

Safeguarding or child protection?

Reviewing progress against the Munro reforms, all contributors to this volume have, to different degrees, considered the impact on the wider multi-agency child protection system. All are in agreement that it is impossible to separate policy and practice about child protection from the legislative context surrounding children at risk across social care, criminal justice, education and health settings. Safeguarding children is the flipside of the coin to public protection and an effective child protection system relies on a shared understanding of risk across health, social care, education and criminal justice agencies (Stephenson and Allen, 2013). In order to protect the most vulnerable children, particularly those at risk of child sexual exploitation (CSE) or going missing (Pearce, Chapter 7; Hedges, Chapter 8), it is essential that front-line services working with children become further integrated.

All contributors share the opinion that rather than a return to a system focused only on a narrow definition of child protection, the safeguarding system post-Munro is one that has been redesigned to support the child's journey from early help through to child protection planning. It is fair to conclude that the new child protection inspection framework (Ofsted, 2013a), alongside revised expectations of local safeguarding children boards (LSCBs) in *Working together* (HM Government, 2013), build on the Munro reforms. Nationally and locally, arguably both have a statutory regulatory role in providing their own assessment of how safe a child protection system is and the extent to which it reflects partnership across social care, health, education and policing.

From this perspective, the Munro reforms provide a coherent national policy for child protection services and set a framework for local implementation.

What is driving child protection policy?

However, the Munro recommendations, important though they have been in redesigning the future of child protection, have not been the only policy driver for the reforms currently under way. There remain three other drivers that determine child protection policy in this country and these underlie all contributions to this book. These are inextricably linked to wider national policy perspectives unique to the current political, social and economic landscape.

First, the pace of change is slow and implementation of the Munro reforms has taken time (Ofsted, 2013a). Despite personal commitment from different children's ministers and the Secretary of State, much has been left to the local level to determine as part of the current administration's commitment to a localist agenda. The government only appointed its first chief social worker in September 2013, revisions to the new *Working together* guidance were delayed until April 2013 and the independent review of social work education led by Martin Narey, intended to boost the numbers of suitably qualified social workers in the system, only commenced in mid-2013. It will be interesting to see whether the government response to the Narey report on social work education (Department for Education, 2014) supports the welcome call for a renewed emphasis on preparing front-line staff for multi-disciplinary working, particularly working within children's services.

This volume demonstrates the urgent need to address why it is so difficult to attract social workers into child protection work and to retain them: solving workforce deficits requires direction from the chief social worker, an active response to Narey's observations and decisive political leadership. Gurrey and Brazil (Chapter 1) outline their ingredients for successful local authority children's services departments leaving no doubt that 'if leadership, learning and development, performance management and supervision, and other key areas of service improvement are not all working together, and influencing each other, the service response to the complexity of the task will never be what it needs to be or as good as it can be' (Chapter 1, p 12).

Having sufficient and properly trained front-line staff is the pillar of system improvement (Ofsted, 2013b). Wright (Chapter 3) asks important questions about who is best to deliver these services and argues that the contracting out of the child protection system to voluntary sector providers, albeit with different expertise and value bases, will bring the necessary experience of relationship-building with vulnerable groups. The Secretary of State has announced government intentions to intervene when children's social care departments are not improving and to place them with such independent providers (Gove, 2013).

Regardless of whether improvement is sector-led or outsourced, services must be able to evidence they can safely protect children. Clifton (Chapter 5) reminds us that all services should be designed to listen to children and their views and experiences placed at the heart of decision-making. Equipping front-line staff with the time to form relationships with families, visit children and adequately reflect on their own judgement requires us to learn from the success of past interventions. It also requires an investment in the 'early offer' and in organisations working together and ensuring that evaluation of other government programmes for vulnerable families impact on child protection delivery (Jones, Chapter 2; White, Morris, Featherstone, Brandon and Thoburn, Chapter 4).

Second, the impact of the economy on public sector children's services, both in terms of reduced funding and reorganisation, has been far-reaching. Contributors to this volume are clear that the child protection system goes further than the work that social workers do and is reliant on forming local relationships across front-line settings. The regulators are also emphatic about this:

> Our inspection evidence demonstrates that good local authorities and their partners understand their area and the needs of families who live there, and commission their services accordingly. The evidence also shows that the weakest child protection services often struggle to secure effective collaboration with other local services. Local authorities must be good partners who create an environment where collaboration thrives. Equally, they must be able to rely on the highest quality response from health services, police, courts and schools. There can be no weak link in the chain. (Ofsted, 2013b, p 10)

The changes to the NHS architecture during 2013/14 are still embedding in some areas of the country, the NHS accountability and assurance framework on children's safeguarding is scant in its detail (NHS Commissioning Board, 2013), and there remain gaps in how the new clinical commissioning groups (CCGs) will resource child protection work alongside NHS providers and NHS England

(National Children's Bureau and NHS Confederation, 2013). The fact that schools have become independent autonomies, many outside local authority control, creates other challenge in securing adequate assurance about safeguarding practice in schools (East Sussex LSCB, 2013).

In January 2014, the Home Office published its report on multi-agency working and information-sharing projects (Home Office, 2014), reinforcing findings from its earlier report (Home Office, 2013) that integrating front-line services helps avoid duplication, enables greater efficiency and allows swift decision-making and sharing of information between police, health and social care professionals. The study concluded that in the areas it observed, there had been a reduction in the risk of 'borderline cases being overlooked without action being taken' (Home Office, 2013). Munro referred to the multi-agency safeguarding hub (MASH) model in her final report and, supported by the adoption of a new single assessment framework at local level, the early findings are promising. For older vulnerable children, sometimes not known to social care departments, such integrated models are seen as the way forward (Hicks, Chapter 6; Pearce, Chapter 7; Hedges, Chapter 8).

Third, the role of the media in this country in influencing child protection policy cannot be underestimated. Jones (Chapter 2) berates the extent to which serious case reviews (SCRs) have become political tools and have distorted public perception about how services protect children. Others in the academic field have expressed similar views (Stafford et al, 2012). There is evidence that, perhaps with the exception of the Munro review, all previous inquiries relating to child protection have been born of high-profile child deaths (Blyth and Solomon, 2012). In November 2013, Annie Hudson, Chief Executive of The College of Social Work, made a plea for more balanced reporting on child deaths, stating:

> There have been some examples of fair and well-researched print and broadcast social work journalism since the Baby Peter case, led by the hard work of social workers and media professionals to communicate the reality of social work in England. Sadly, however, there

have also been some truly insensitive and unethical examples too. (Hudson, 2013)

Where next for child protection?

The chapters in this book reflect the diversity of challenges facing the child protection system and the hardships facing some children who require protection from all forms of maltreatment. The volume concludes that the Munro review has been a real driver for system improvement across the child protection system. All contributors reinforce that much child protection in many parts of the country is strong and effective, albeit 'it seems that child protection is at a crucial cusp' (Jones, Chapter 2, p 48). At national and local level, there has been a visible commitment to take on board the Munro reforms since 2011 and her findings have become a benchmark for judging effectiveness (Ofsted, 2013a). However, there remains a significant journey to ensure that all child protection services are safe and this will require commitment across local authorities, the new NHS, education providers and policing. It will involve a robust and realistic review of the role of LSCBs and a persistent preoccupation with improvement, and must be supported by strong local and central political leadership. Most importantly, any further reform of the child protection system must see a shift not only in reporting the tragic deaths of children but also in documenting a greater understanding of the challenges facing many children and young people at risk and how best to provide services in this country to protect them. Only as the remainder of this decade unfolds, will we really know the legacy of the Munro reforms.

References

Blyth, M. and Solomon, E. (2012) *Effective safeguarding: what next after Munro?*, Bristol: Policy Press.

Department for Education (2004) *Every child matters*, London: The Stationery Office.

Department for Education (2014) *Making the education of social workers consistently effective: Report of Sir Martin Narey's independent review of the education of children's social workers*, London: DfE.

East Sussex LSCB (Local Safeguarding Children Board) (2013) *SCR: Child G*, East Sussex LSCB.

Gove, M. (2013) 'Getting it right for children in need', Speech to NSPCC, 12 November.

HM Government (2013) *Working together to safeguard children. A guide to inter-agency working to safeguard and promote the welfare of children*, London: The Stationery Office.

Home Office (2013) *Multi-agency working and information sharing projects*, London: HM Government.

Hudson, A. (2013) Speech to NSPCC, November.

Munro, E. (2011) *The Munro review of child protection. Final report: a child-centred system*, London: The Stationery Office.

Munro, E. (2012) *The Munro review of child protection. Progress report: moving towards a child-centred system*, London: The Stationery Office.

National Children's Bureau and NHS Confederation (2013) *Child health in the new NHS*, London: NCB.

NHS Commissioning Board (2013) *National Accountability Framework:*, London: The Stationery Office.

Ofsted (Office for Standards in Education) (2013a) *Framework and evaluation schedule for the inspection of services for children in need of help and protection, children looked after and care leavers (single inspection framework) and reviews of local safeguarding children boards*, Manchester: Ofsted.

Ofsted (2013b) *Social care annual report, 2012/13*, Manchester: Ofsted.

Stafford, A., Parton, N., Vincent, S. and Smith, C. (2012) *Child protection systems in the UK*, London: Jessica Kingsley Publishers.

Stephenson, M. and Allen, R. (2013) *Youth justice: challenges to practice*, London: Unitas.

Index